Accounting
for
Management
Control

The Chapman & Hall Series in Accounting and Finance

Consulting editors
John Perrin, Emeritus Professor of the University of Warwick and Price Waterhouse Fellow in Public Sector Accounting at the University of Exeter; Richard M.S. Wilson, Professor of Management Control in the School of Finance and Information at the Queen's University of Belfast and L.C.L. Skerratt, Professor of Financial Accounting at the University of Manchester.

H.M. Coombs and D.E. Jenkins
Public Sector Financial Management

J.C. Drury
Management and Cost Accounting (2nd edn)
(Also available: **Students' Manual, Teachers' Manual**)

C.R. Emmanuel, D.T. Otley and K. Merchant
Accounting for Management Control (2nd edn)
(Also available: **Teachers' Guide**)

C.R. Emmanuel, D.T. Otley and K. Merchant
Readings in Accounting for Management Control

D. Henley, C. Holtham, A. Likierman and J. Perrin
Public Sector Accounting and Financial Control (3rd edn)

R.C. Laughlin and R.H. Gray
Financial Accounting; method and meaning
(Also available: **Teachers' Guide**)

G.A. Lee
Modern Financial Accounting (4th edn)
(Also available: **Solutions Manual**)

T.A. Lee
Income Value Measurement (3rd edn)

T.A. Lee
Company Financial Reporting (2nd edn)

T.A. Lee
Cash Flow Accounting

S.P. Lumby
Investment Appraisal and Financing Decisions (4th edn)
(Also available: **Students' Manual**)

A.G. Puxty and J.C. Dodds
Financial Management: method and meaning (2nd edn)
(Also available: **Teachers' Guide**)

J.M. Samuels, F.M. Wilkes and R.E. Brayshaw
Management of Company Finance (5th edn)
(Also available: **Students' Manual**)

B. Spaul and B. Williams
IT and Accounting: the impact of information technology)

R.M.S. Wilson and Wai Fong Chua
Managerial Accounting: method and meaning
(Also available: **Teachers' Guide**)

Accounting
for
Management
Control

SECOND EDITION

Teachers' Manual

Clive Emmanuel
University of Glasgow

David Otley
University of Lancaster

and

Kenneth Merchant
University of Southern California

CHAPMAN & HALL
University and Professional Division

London · New York · Tokyo · Melbourne · Madras

UK	Chapman & Hall, 2–6 Boundary Row, London SE1 8HN
USA	Chapman & Hall, 29 West 35th Street, New York NY10001
JAPAN	Chapman & Hall Japan, Thomson Publishing Japan, Hirakawacho Nemoto Building, 7F, 1-7-11 Hirakawa-cho, Chiyoda-ku, Tokyo 102
AUSTRALIA	Chapman & Hall Australia, Thomas Nelson Australia, 102 Dodds Street, South Melbourne, Victoria 3205
INDIA	Chapman & Hall India, R. Seshadri, 32 Second Main Road, CIT East, Madras 600 035

First edition 1985
Reprinted twice in 1986, twice in 1987
Second edition 1991

© 1991 Clive Emmanuel, David Otley and Kenneth Merchant

Printed in Great Britain by St Edmundsbury Press, Bury St Edmunds, Suffolk

ISBN 0 412 43070 3

British Library Cataloguing in Publication Data available

Library of Congress Cataloguing-in Publication Data available

Contents

Preface

Accounting for Management Control has become a widely used text, with most British undergraduates taking an accounting degree, being exposed to it at some time during their studies. It has also been used in a considerable number of other countries, including the USA. In addition to its use at undergraduate level, it has also proved helpful in teaching management control on MBA and other specialist Masters courses.

The second edition has seen the addition of some new chapters, a selection of case studies and a greater number of end-of-chapter exercises. It was therefore thought that it would be helpful to expand the original photocopied notes for teachers into a fully developed Teachers' Manual. This book is the result. It contains brief notes on all the end-of-chapter exercises, together with full solutions to all the quantitative questions. These notes also include some suggestions for further reading in the journal literature on the question topics. In addition, teaching notes are provided for all the case studies. However, it should be emphasized that these notes are not exhaustive; they represent just one approach to the issues raised, and many teachers will find that they prefer to use the material offered in other ways.

We would also draw attention to the availability of a collection of selected journal articles designed to complement the original text, and to allow students to have access to some of the more important journal literature underlying the main text. Entitled *Readings in Accounting for Management Control,* this is available from mid-1991. We hope that both this manual and the associated book of readings will provide a helpful resource for the many teachers we know who have found our text well-suited to their needs.

Clive Emmanuel, University of Glasgow
Kenneth Merchant, University of Southern California
David Otley, Lancaster University

USE OF TEXT

This text has been used successfully on a variety of courses, including undergraduate accounting courses and postgraduate management control systems courses.

For undergraduate use, it should be used jointly with (or be preceded by) material on intermediate management accounting techniques, such as those presented by Horngren and Foster (1987) or Drury (1988). It is possibly most straightforward for students to have completed a course on the decision-making aspects of accounting data beforehand, but to study divisional performance measurement and transfer pricing in the current course. Given that some basic groundwork has been covered, it is possible to complete the text during a one-term undergraduate course. Part One should be restricted to 25% of the course; Part Two should be a summary of previous work, with perhaps an emphasis on financial planning, and take no more than 25% of the time. This leaves about 50% of the time available for Part Three. The Permaclean case is best used with Part Two; the remainder of the cases can then be used with Part Three, with Altex being kept as a summary case.

For a postgraduate accounting course, this text is perhaps best used in conjunction with Macintosh (1985) which goes into more depth in the research literature. Alternatively, students can be assigned readings from the accounting journals, especially from Accounting, Organisations and Society. Students' greater familiarity with accounting techniques is often compensated for by the fact that they are less used to the approach adopted, and more time may be usefully assigned to Parts One and Two in comparison to Part Three.

For a management control systems course, this text is better if supplemented with more case studies, and perhaps used in conjunction with another text. Anthony, Dearden and Bedford (1984) is universally popular and contains many good cases, although the text is weak. Maciariello (1984) has a stronger text, although having a marked cybernetic flavour, and an adequate selection of additional cases. A balance of case classes, workshops on assigned exercises, and conceptual discussion sessions work well within a course having 30-40 hours of class contact time.

SOLUTION NOTES

These notes are intended to give guidance to teachers concerning the types of answer that are expected to the end-of-chapter exercises. They represent one possible answer; in many cases there are alternative answers that could be equally appropriate. Where a reference to a journal article is given, this provides a link with the section of the text thought most appropriate. A reference under "Further reading" provides some background to one of the main issues raised by a question; students would not normally be expected to have read this reference, although it would be a good starting point for a more extended discussion of the topic. Where only a short-form reference is given the full reference appears in the reference list in the text.

References: Anthony, R.A., Dearden J. and Bedford, N.M. (1984) Management Control Systems (5th edition), Irwin.

Maciariello, J.A. (1984) Management Control Systems, Prentice-Hall.

CHAPTER 1

ACCOUNTING FOR ORGANIZATIONAL CONTROL

1.   This question focuses on a major decision that the student is likely to have made in the not-too-distant past. When presenting a description of such a decision, it is likely that the student will describe it in a fairly rational manner, i.e. by defining objectives, outlining possible solutions, selecting the best solution and putting it into effect. Allow this to happen and obtain descriptions of different decisions from different students without too much prompting. Then turn to the second decision that still has to be taken. Again obtain descriptions, which this time are likely to be much less rational. Focus on the processes of defining objectives for the decision (often multiple and conflicting): deciding upon what possible courses of action exist, and of obtaining information on these, predicting the likely outcomes of alternative courses of action in terms of the objectives previously described (usually very difficult to do); and selecting the 'best'. This will usually look much less rational due to:

(a)   problems in selecting and weighting objectives

(b)   information problems in developing alternative courses of action

(c)   weaknesses in available predictive models of outcomes.

Indeed objectives will tend to emerge and develop as the decision-making process proceeds. It is only necessary to weight objectives when a conflict occurs, rather than resolving conflicts before they actually happen. New objectives emerge when a choice has to be made between otherwise equally good alternatives; old objectives may be dropped when it is apparent no alternative considered achieves them.

3

Reference: Lindblom, C.E. (1959)

Further reading: Harrison, E.F. (1975) <u>The Managerial Decision-Making Process</u>, Boston, Houghton Mifflin.

2. A perfectly competitive economic market is perhaps the best source of examples of how a set of individuals, each pursuing their own self-interests, can produce resultant behaviour that maximizes the total social welfare of the group (despite its relatively infrequent occurrence in practice). A useful, smaller scale, example is the class being taught by the tutor. Students can be asked what the objectives of the class as a whole are. Some vague notions of learning may be advanced, but most objectives suggested are usually individual objectives (e.g. passing an exam) not shared, group objectives. (Suppose the pass rate was set in advance, such that only 50% would pass?) In any case, if the <u>tutor</u> is included in the group an overall objective is almost impossible to define. Yet regular patterns of group behaviour occur. This can be quite satisfactorily explained in utilitarian terms: each student individually wished to pass the examination, and sees attendance at the tutorial as a means to that end; the tutor wishes to earn a salary and attends so that this occurs. This is a purely utilitarian analysis. Now apply this to business examples, bearing in mind that there will also be normative and coercive elements in most real situations, (e.g. compare and contrast why the managing director and shop floor worker turn up to work on time every day).

Reference: Etzioni, A. (1961)

Further reading: Beynon, M. (1973)

3.   A wide range of information that would be helpful can be suggested. Most of the quantitative information usually relates to the construction of an economic demand curve relating price charged to quantity sold, and to any cost changes consequent upon production volume changing. However, in practice, it is not usually possible to construct anything like a complete economic analysis and serious consideration is given only to limited number of alternatives. Important, but more qualitative information would include:

(a) inter-relationships with other products

(b) links between price and perceived quality of product

(c) impact on competitors, and their likely response

(d) short-term vs long-term considerations.

Many assumptions will, in practice, be made in conducting this type of analysis, but a degree of learning can be obtained by a careful collection of relevant information after the event. Did customers react in the expected way? How did competitors respond? Such information needs to be collated with the original assumptions, not to show how poor a decision was taken, but to help improve the quality of the next decision.

Reference: Arnold (1973)

Further reading: Sizer, J. (1979)

4.   This question requires that the model of control developed in the chapter and applied there to the control of a vehicle, is applied to other systems. It is most easily applied to simple, mechanical systems, and the student gains confidence in doing this, but it is then necessary to encourage it to be applied to human systems. Again it is probably best to consider a simple social situation involving just two or three people, before progressing to a business situation.   The analysis raises many

problems. These include the question of organizational objectives (which should have been dealt with prior to setting this question) which can be characterized as multiple, conflicting and ambiguous; the question of what is measured as a surrogate for actual performance; and the selection of control actions. But central to any control system is a predictive model, for without prediction there can be no control. What is crucial to the effectiveness of any control system is the accuracy of its predictions as to the effect of proposed corrective actions. In simple systems, the predictive model may be in-built into the system itself (e.g. thermostatic control of central heating); in human systems, different people may well have different predictive models. In many situations it is worth asking whether an organizational predictive model actually exists, and where it can be located. The final part of the question if included to stimulate the thought that improvements to predictive models can only occur if the experience of poor control is used constructively.

Reference: Otley, D.T. and Berry, A.J. (1980)

Further reading: Argyris, C. and Schon, D (1978) Organizational Learning, Addison-Wesley.

5.   This is necessarily true, although its corrollary is that learning would not be required if we already knew how to do things right! Nevertheless, our understanding is sufficiently imperfect that learning is a vital part of any control system. Again, the important lesson is that the experience of doing things badly is not something to be forgotten or used solely to attach blame, but can be used positively to improve future performance. However, there are other pre-conditions:

   (a) Rapid feedback on (reliably-measured) results is essential. Learning does not occur when we are ignorant of our performance.

   (b) Desired standards of performance need to be communicated and accepted.

(c) There is a need for the motivation to do better, whether because of an internal desire or because of an externally-imposed system of performance evaluation, where rewards are attached to results.

Much of this discussion can seem abstract to students with limited work experience when applied to a business situation. For that reason, it is suggested they apply it to the design of the course they are currently taking. No doubt they will raise issues of lack of feedback about performance expected and that actually attained, its timeliness and its quality as a means of learning how to improve. This is one tutorial where the teacher may learn more than the pupil!

Reference: Locke, E.A. (1968)

Further reading: Lawler, E.E. III (1973)

6. The examples chosen are designed to illustrate the progressive difficulty in designing adequate control systems as jobs become more complex, subject to greater environmental uncertainty and involve a greater time span of discretion.

(a) Speed of production is determined by the spread of the production line, provided the worker keeps up and completes the whole job correctly. Thus, a quality control check is the major control necessary. It is also necessary to consider how poor quality should be dealt with – in some cases a worker would be required to rectify his own defects, but his is not possible on a production line. Perhaps an incentive bonus for good quality is required, but how do you check the quality inspectors' work?

(b) Sales are what matters here, together with price obtained if the salesman is given discretion in allowing sales discounts. But how do you set a standard or quota for a given period: comparison with other periods, or the results of other salesmen in different towns may not be relevant. The usual solution is to make the salesman's remuneration heavily dependent upon sales made, although this provides an incentive for the salesman to use tactics which may not be in the company's best long-term interests.

(c) The problem here is that a useful discovery may take several years, and that the person in the best position to assess whether the most appropriate work is being done may well be the scientist himself, and his peers. Perhaps the best that can be done is to provide adequate resources and employ a group of people motivated to make discoveries (possibly because of status gained by scientific publication). Most efforts to stimulate quick results are likely to prove counter-productive in the longer-term.

(d) A wide range of performance indicators can be devised (e.g. profit, ROCE, profit/employee, costs as % of sales etc. etc.), but the problem is what standard of comparison is to be used (e.g. past performance, budgeted performance, what is being achieved elsewhere). Further, a managing director should also be concerned with planning for the longer-term; this can only be fully assessed long into the future when it is too late to correct any mistakes that may have been made.

Reference: Drucker, P. (1964b)

Further reading: Tricker, R.I. (1976) <u>Management Information and Control Systems</u>, New York, Wiley.

7. This can be a very productive exercise, as it relates control processes to a familiar situation. Major points include:

(a) Multiple and conflicting objectives having different time-spans (e.g. learn to pass an exam <u>vs</u> appreciate a subject).

(b) How often should performance be measured (e.g. final exams only <u>vs</u> some coursework assessment <u>vs</u> weekly assessment)? What is the implicit or explicit standard used (e.g. other students in group <u>vs</u> some objective measure of learning achieved).

(c) Who is doing the controlling? (i.e. is the system for staff to monitor learning or is it for students to monitor and control their own progress?) What is the implicit model of human behaviour used in the control system? (e.g. Theory X or Theory Y?) What do we know about how people learn?

(d) From the teacher's point of view, what can be done to change student behaviour? (e.g. different styles of running a tutorial, such as a random choice of student to present the exercise set).

Having identified the major issues and suggested some improvements, do the students feel they would like to work <u>under</u> the system they have designed? What is the role of the <u>controllee</u> in the design of control systems?

Further reading: Entwistle, N. and Hounsell, D. (1975) 'How Students Learn' in <u>Readings in Higher Education 1</u>, University of Lancaster.

8. This can stimulate an interesting discussion. Possible answers are:

(a) From their articles of association. However most companies have extremely non-specific articles for good legal reasons.

(b) By asking them. But who should you ask? Different answers would no doubt be obtained from the managing director, other functional directors and the man who sweeps the factory floor. Are we obtaining individual objectives, the objectives of the ruling coalition, or organizational objectives?

(c) From the corporate plan. But the relevance of the plan to what is actually done is often suspect. Corporate plans often seem to be symbolic documents rather than guides to action.

(d) By observing what the organization actually does. One cannot deny that actual behaviour is good evidence, but it is not possible to infer objectives solely from behaviour. Is a company that makes a loss doing it intentionally, or is its objective to be profitable? Evidence can be obtained in all these ways, but it cannot lead to definitive conclusions. Indeed if organizational objectives are multiple, conflicting, ambiguous and changing over time, can expect more? This discussion can lead directly into 'garbage-can' models of decision-making if required.

Reference: Cyert, R.M. and March, J.G. (1963)
Further reading: March, J.G. and Olsen, J.G. (1976)

9.   A given plan of action has a multitude of different results. Thus different participants can each achieve part of their own objectives by being involved in a joint plan of action even though they might find it difficult to agree on overall objectives. In some circumstances (e.g. normatively-oriented groups) it may be necessary for

participants to express agreement with some supposedly shared objectives, even though their motivation for being involved could be for quite different reasons. Voluntary organizations provide a happy hunting ground for examples!

The counter-examples usually involve different people holding different and conflicting predictive models. Thus, all may be able to agree on the desirability of pursuing a particular objective, but predict very different consequences for implementing a given course of action.

Earl and Hopwood's (1981) analysis contains both these elements. Uncertainty in objectives allows objectives to be ambiguous and not fully agreed; uncertainty in cause–effect relationships is equivalent to having a poor predictive model.

Reference: Earl, M. and Hopwood, A.G. (1981)

10. Discovering what the goals of an organizations actually are (independently of examining measures of performance) can be difficult, but some general goals can usually be set down. Specific measures of performance are usually easily identified; what then needs to be done is to examine the ways in which good results (as measured) can be obtained without assisting goal attainment, or possibly in a way which is counter-productive to goal attainment (i.e. dysfunctional behaviour).

A tutorial group can provide good examples. General goals of student learning can be proposed and the means intended to achieve these goals examined (e.g. preparation of tutorial work, course-work assessment, examinations). Many specific performance measures may be detrimental to the wider objective of learning.

The major problems are raised by organizations having ill-defined objectives. Here, specific performance measures are used as surrogates for objectives and many convey strong messages, but possibly inappropriate messages, to participants. Equally, the lack of measurement of espoused objectives can lead to the message being received that such objectives are not really important.

CHAPTER 2

THE DESIGN OF ORGANIZATIONS

(Note: Reference can be made to the texts on organization theory recommended in the chapter)

1. The objective of this question is to relate the rather abstract material of the chapter to concrete examples drawn from the student's own experience. We all come into contact with large organizations every day, so we all have some relevant experience, even if little of it comes directly from working for such an organization. Vacation jobs, part-time work and voluntary work also usually provide fruitful sources of experience. Some examples, and insights drawn from them include:

    (a) Dealing with the Department of Social Security as a client gives direct experience of a large bureaucracy designed to control employee behaviour by a series of detailed rules. Exceptions to the rules are passed up the hierarchy; clients combining sets of characteristics normally dealt with by two separate departments are also a problem and cannot be dealt with by standard procedures.

    (b) Student and other voluntary organizations are often a good example of more flexible structures with a great deal of informal communication (or lack of it!). They also illustrate different degrees of commitment from different participants to a greater extent than most work organizations having full-time employees.

(c) The marketing of home computers provides a current example of the need for organizations to adapt to a rapidly changing environment, involving both technological change and changing consumer tastes. Open systems theory seems to offer the best basis for analysis.

Further reading: Khandwalla, P.N. (1977)

2.   Again, this question seeks to draw on common experience to provide examples to illustrate the chapter material. Characteristics of chain stores that may be observed include:

(a) range of merchandise offered

(b) differences allowed in the same store in different locations (e.g. range, price, layout, etc.)

(c) salary structure of employees (e.g. commission element)

(d) accounting systems as reflected in billing procedures, refund procedures, special orders, credit card usage, etc.

These, and many other, factors can be related to the target market that the store aims to serve (e.g. mass merchandising of standard products vs supplying to individual customer demand).

Further reading: Chandler, A.D. (1962)

3.   Most of the theories of management expounded in the chapter have been developed specifically in relation to business organizations (or derived from military organization). It can be useful to try to extend them to other types of organization to explore their limitations and weaknesses.

(a) Hospitals in the UK display many of the management problems that arise when services are not paid for by the user at the time of use. In addition there are problems of authority with a dual structure of command (doctors

14

with responsibility for patients; administrators responsible for services/finance). A useful contrast is provided by private hospitals which do not have the former problem.

(b) Universities are a good example of organizations where the quantity and quality of their output is not easily measurable. This may be possible to some extent for their teaching functions, but research is notoriously difficult to quantify in this way. The balance between two such different activities involving the same staff also raises problems. Management of universities has traditionally been by consensus with a strong emphasis on bottom-up planning, although recent expenditure cuts in the UK have led to demands for a more 'business-like' style of management.

(c) Postal services and telecommunications are invariably subject to state control, probably due to a combination of their importance and the economies that occur if such services are provided by a monopoly. This leads to a uniformity of provision that requires consideration of how to balance quality of service with cost.

(d) Local government is concerned with providing local public services financed by local taxes (although central financing is a major element in UK local government). Day-to-day management is by employed officers in the UK (although often by elected officers often in the USA) controlled by elected representatives. This produces a contrast between those having power but restricted knowledge and those having detailed knowledge but nominally subject to the elected representatives.

Further reading: Dermer, J. (1977).

15

4. The contrast of business organizations with military organizations is an important one because of the way in which much conventional wisdom on organizations has tended to be derived from military analogies (often due to ex-soldiers taking up business appointments). Military organizations face a hostile environment that attempts to gain the advantage of surprise; it is necessary for the organization to continue to function even when it is heavily damaged. Hence heavy redundancy and hierarchical systems of authority are built into the structure. Such conditions are rare in business, except in the most highly competitive environments, and even there the orgnization is likely to remain intact, except insofar as key managers are 'headhunted'. The 'line and staff' of military organizations have clear benefits, but they also have deficiences, even in military situations. Examples of the lack of co-operation between the three services, each independently organized, have been well documented on numerous occasions. In less threatening situations, organizational forms better suited to developing consensus and managing interdependencies have been constructed. Whilst lessons can be learnt from military organization, it should not be taken as the sole model for business organizations.

Further reading: Lawrence, P.R. and J.W. Lorsch (1967b)

5. The contingency theory of organizational structure suggests that the most appropriate form of organization is dependent upon certain situational variables, most notably the nature of the external environment (and particularly its inherent uncertainty) and the nature of the task being undertaken. The theory developed out of empirical studies, some of which had set out to discover universal rules for organizational structure (e.g. Woodward, 1958). There are fairly clear-cut results that indicate that particular forms of technology (e.g. unit, mass and process production)

and certain environments (e.g. stable <u>versus</u> rapidly changing) are best dealt with by certain organizational forms, although this is not to deny the existence of managerial choice.

The contingency theory of management accounting has tended to take the above results as given, and to use environment, technology and organizational structure itself as contingent variables to explain the differing forms of management accounting information systems that exist. Despite the reasonable assumption that the form of an accounting system is situation dependent, empirical results have been disappointing. This has been due to a number of factors:

(a) the way in which the studies have been conducted, and particularly, the choice of relatively homogeneous samples of companies studied

(b) the use of organizational structure as a contingent variable when it is inter-dependent with accounting system design

(c) the neglect of important variables such as corporate strategy, and the effect of ownership in imposing accounting systems on subsidiaries

(d) the relatively small effect AIS design is likely to have an overall performance.

Reference   Otley, D.T. (1980)

Further reading: Macintosh, N.B. <u>The Social Software of Accounting and Information Systems</u>, New York, Wiley, 1985.

6.   With a perishable product or service, time is a critical factor. Last minute decisions have to be taken, and there may not be time to refer them to higher levels in the hierarchy. There seems to be two different organizational responses to the problem. One is to develop highly efficient centralized decision-making processes, usually involving significant investment in real-time information systems. The

17

booking systems of airlines, and some hotels, are examples. The second is to devolve considerable authority to managers on-the-spot, dealing directly with customers to take decisions. Thus, hotel receptionists may be able to negotiate on price with customers who turn up late at night, but who appear prepared to continue along the road if the price is not right. Travel agents may discount holidays themselves if they have responsibility for a block booking. Interesting contrasts develop when companies which have responded in different ways to the problem compete head-on.

Further reading: Pfeffer, J. (1982)

7.   There are several possible means of coping with high levels of uncertainty. These essentially reduce to:

    (a) Maintaining flexibility to deal with the unexpected. For example, a fashion clothes manufacturer may organize to be able to produce quickly in response to market trends.

    (b) Attempting to predict outcomes by investing in planning, information systems and the gathering of market intelligence. For example, fashion houses may employ people to visit fashionable night-spots to discover trends as they originate.

    (c) Attempting to affect the environment. For example, fashion houses may agree amongst themselves on the colours that will be promoted in the coming season.

    (d) Avoiding those parts of the environment that exhibit too much uncertainty and concentrating on more predictable areas.

Reference: Lowe, E.A. and Machin, J.L.F. (1983), Chapter 6

Further reading: Mintzberg, H. (1979)

8. Decentralization is the delegation of decision-making to low levels in the organization; divisionalization is the devolution of authority for the running of a business entity to second-level management. Within the division itself, management may be highly centralized.

However different decisions may display different patterns of decentralization, possibly with operating and marketing decisions being decentralized, but with financial decisions being centralized. A firm is decentralized to the extent that many important decisions are taken at lower levels, but different firms may be decentralized in different ways.

Divisionalization refers to the decentralization of a wide range of operating and financial decisions (with the possible exception of capital investment decisions) to one level below top corporate management. However, it does not specify what occurs below that level. For example it is possible to have a divisionalized firm in which each decision is highly decentralized. Thus divisionalization represents one form of decentralization.

The major <u>accounting</u> problems in constructing a profit-based measure of divisional performance are:

(a) definition and measurement of capital employed

(b) choice of an appropriate cost of capital

(c) making allowance for the different riskiness of different divisions

(d) costing of centrally provided services and the allocation of non-divisional costs

(e) choice of transfer prices for goods and services transferred between divisions.

The most commonly used accounting-based measures of performance for divisionalized firms are accounting profit and returns on investment. However if divisional managers are evaluated on either of these measures they may be motivated to undertake activities not in the best interest of the overall organization. For example, to increase profit a divisional manager may take on low yielding yet profitable activities; to maintain a high return on investment a divisional manager may neglect to implement adequately yielding activities that have a return on investment below his current average return. To avoid these potential problems, it has been suggested that accounting profits should be adjusted by a charge for the capital employed in a division to give a measure named 'residual income', i.e.

Residual income =   Accounting income less (Capital employed x cost of capital %)

The use of such a measure requires all the problems involved in assessing accounting income to be overcome (e.g. overhead allocation, product costing, asset valuation and depreciation, inventory policy, inflation adjustment). Additionally it requires both capital employed and the true percentage cost of that capital to be assessed. The most major problem here is in assessing the cost of equity capital employed in a division, making due allowance for its risk characteristics.

Finally, in order to measure income for a division which is engaged in internal trade with other divisions in the same company, transfer prices must be set for items which are internally traded. Inappropriate transfer prices will lead to miscalculation of divisional profits, increasing those of some divisions at the expense of others. The setting of transfer prices is probably the most critical problem to be solved in setting up profit-based performance measures for divisions of a multidivisional company.

Reference: See Chapter 9 for more extensive discussion

Further reading: Solomons, D. (1965)

9. The control model developed in Chapter 1 indicates two different roles for information. The first is measuring what actually occurs and comparing it with objectives, generating what Vickers (1967) has termed a 'mis-match' signal. Having drawn attention to the fact that results differ from plans, the accounting information may have served its purpose and other information used to generated solutions to the problem identified. The second role of accounting information is to inform the predictive model, especially with regard to the financial consequences of plans of action.

The second use is seen most obviously in the budget process. The financial consequences of plans we calculated and then passed to senior management for their evaluation. Typically, the overall financial consequences are seen to be inadequate and changes to the plans are required to be explored until a more desirable set of outcomes is forecast. At worst, only the financial estimates are adjusted, with no change to the underlying plans.

The contingency theory of AIS design can probably be widened to encompass MCS design. What is appropriate in a stable and predictable environment is probably not suitable for a rapidly changing environment with a high level of uncertainty. Here, speed of response and flexibility are likely to dominate accurate, but time-consuming, considered responses.

Reference: Vickers, G. (1967)

CHAPTER 3

INDIVIDUAL MOTIVATION AND INCENTIVES

1. The objective of this question is to explore the similarities and differences between the incentives that would encourage different people to work harder. To the extent that similarities exist, it is possible to develop general theories of motivation that may apply to a given group of people, such as those of Maslow, McGregor and Herzberg. To the extent that differences exist, the model has to be adjusted to the individual, as in the expectancy theory of motivation. It is usually the case that incentives that would be highly effective for one person prove to be ineffective, or even counter-productive, for another.

It should also be noted that the effect of an incentive is related both to how much of it currently exists and the current level of effort. Somebody already working hard may require greater incentives for extra effort; indeed such extra incentives may be harmful if they produce levels of activation that cannot be translated into productive activity.

The design of a reward system that rewards goal attainment is straight-forward. However, designing it not to reward inappropriate behaviour is more difficult. Once a specific reward system has been designed, it is useful to set the group the task of discovering what behaviours will be encouraged (by being rewarded) that are not desirable.

Reference: Burgoyne (1975)

Further reading: Hopwood, A.G. (1974).

2. It is a sad fact of life that hard work does not necessarily provide high attainment. This may be because of a lack of ability or experience, because the effort is mis-directed, or because external circumstances change. For most tasks there is only a probabilistic relationship between effort and attainment. Thus if only attainment is rewarded, this can appear to be very unfair. Payment by results will motivate only if results are roughly proportional to effort, but this carries the corresponding risk that the effort may be mis-directed, and that new ways of achieving results are not explored.

It is illuminating to examine compensation schemes at both senior and shop-floor levels in an organization. Senior managers may be rewarded substantially by results (although often retaining a substantial base salary), especially in the USA, by means of stock options and bonus payments. However, it has been argued that such schemes encourage a short-term orientation and a lack of concern about strategic planning. Shop-floor workers are also often paid by results in piece-work and incentive bonus schemes. However, such schemes often have a float, below which earnings cannot fall (to protect the worker against lack of availability of work for reasons outside of his control) and also a ceiling. Even if there is no formal ceiling, workers may informally restrict output to avoid management from re-setting the performance standards.

Reference: Yetton, P. (1976)

3. Herzberg's results are difficult to replicate unless a similar form of questioning is used i.e. can the respondent recollect incidents about which he felt particularly good or bad? This suggests that two-factor theory is more applicable to the extremes of motivation, rather than to marginal changes. However, the approach is worth trying

23

with a group to see if similar sets of commonalities occur. The main purpose of the question is to provoke a discussion of Herzberg's limitations, and to compare his theory with others discussed in the Chapter.

Reference : Herzberg, F. et al (1959)

Further reading: Campbell, J.P. et al (1970)

4. This question focuses attention on the role of shared values and norms on the process of individual motivation. Most of the theories outlined in the Chapter regard the person being motivated as an individual, unaffected by the groups to which he belongs. This is evidently a great simplification and many examples of the effects of social groups on work behaviour exist. For example, the practices of US and Japanese employers contrast markedly, with the former stressing the individual and the latter the working group and local community.

Content theories are evidently culture-specific and have generally been developed in the USA. They may thus be less applicable to Western Europe and have little validity in other, radically different, cultures. Process theories may be easier to translate across cultural boundaries, although they still stress the individual rather than the group. Other motivational mechanisms based on the group exist; for example, until the 1950s it was the usual practice in the UK coal industry to pay the working group a sum of money based on their output, but to leave it to the group to determine the proportions in which this lump sum was to be shared.

Discussion groups containing members from different cultures are a rich source of varied examples relevant to this question.

Further reading: Handy, C. (1978)

5. Despite their good intentions, the effect of most systems of mass education is to produce a variety of undesirable behaviour. A system based on final examinations does not motivate high effort in the early to middle stages of a course. The addition of assessed coursework leads to a neglect of unassessed work. The more complex the rules, the more it seems to encourage inappropriate behaviour.

Rather than discussing such broad issues for too long, it is usually helpful to focus on a specific topic, such as contributing to tutorial discussions. Lack of contribution is usually caused by a combination of:

(a) lack of preparation

(b) not wishing to appear foolish in front of others or the instructor

(c) a group norm of not wishing to appear better than the rest of the group.

Examine the effects of alternative methods of running the tutorial (e.g. choosing at random a student to present the topic each week). I have run a case class where a coursework mark was obtained on the basis of:

(a) attendance

(b) contributions to discussions

(c) marking of work produced in a 5 minute essay set at a (random) stage in the case discussion.

This produced a high level of involvement, but caused considerable stress for a number of students.

Further reading: McGregor, D. (1960)

6. This question is a vehicle to ensure that students have understood the basic components of the expectancy model and can apply them to a concrete situation. Care should be taken to focus on each element of the model i.e.:

(a) Intrinsic valences – not necessarily negative for academic work; it is often enjoyable once begun. Even if the work itself has a negative valence, task accomplishment is usually satisfying.

(b) Extrinsic valences – the rewards and penalties associated with working hard.

(c) Probability that extra effort will lead to more successful task attainment.

(d) Probability that successful task attainment will produce a valued reward – consider both short-term and long-term rewards.

Changes that seem desirable from the point of view of one person often seem less desirable to others. Explore the reasons for such differences of opinion.

Reference: Otley, D.T., Autumn 1982, 'Budgets and Managerial Motivation', Journal of General Management, pp. 26-42.

Further reading: Gilbert, T.F., 1978, Human Competence: Engineering Worthy Performance, McGraw-Hill.

7. The accounting literature talks about setting challenging targets to motivate good performance. However, Hofstede notes that what is challenging depends upon both the situation and the person involved. Often, the person responsible for setting the target knows less about the situation being managed than the person being given the target. Further, different people respond to targets in different ways. This problem has been analysed from several different perspectives, including motivational theory, agency theory and accounting. Further detail is included in Chapter 7, but what is important at this stage is to discover the general issues.

Participation in target setting is essential to the development and monitoring of effective motivational targets, but this can be a two-edged weapon allowing the subordinate to affect his superior's perceptions by the selective release of information. Again, a practical example would be sought from the educational environment (e.g. setting work targets etc).

Reference: Birnberg, J.G. et al (1983)

Further reading: Otley, D.T. (1977)

8.   Auditing is a good example of a basically routine task, where the major decisions necessary are taken by the senior manager. The audit clerk is primarily responsible for carrying out well-defined and specific tasks. However, the difficulty of these tasks and the time necessary to perform them varies from situation to situation, and this information is known only to the person actually performing them. Auditing is usually organized in a mechanistic and bureacratic manner (with huge procedural manuals); motivational theories seem fairly crude and most akin to McGregor's Theory X at this level.

A major organizational control is often the time-sheet, necessary for billing clients, but also used as a control over audit clerks. Most such sheets have space for unproductive time, but there is a strong organizational norm as to how much time can be entered here; otherwise it has to be re-allocated to clients! It is often observed that audit clerks may choose to finish a task in their own time rather than record excess hours over budget on the time sheet. This may be beneficial to the organization in the short–term, but causes its planning information to go badly astray.

9.

Simon Smooth

£000's	Sales			Remuneration		
	Target	Actual	Commission	Bonus	Basic	Total
July	40	20	0.2		0.2	0.4
August	22	50	0.5	1.4	0.2	2.1
September	55	30	0.3		0.2	0.5
October	33	60	0.6	1.35	0.2	2.15
November	66	20	0.2		0.2	0.4
December	22	60	0.6	1.9	0.2	2.7
Total	238	240	2.4	4.65	1.2	8.25

Percival Plodder

£000's	Sales			Remuneration		
	Target	Actual	Commission	Bonus	Basic	Total
July	40	40	0.40		0.2	0.6
August	44	46	0.46	0.1	0.2	0.76
September	50.6	36	0.36		0.2	0.56
October	39.6	42	0.42	0.12	0.2	0.74
November	46.2	38	0.38		0.2	0.58
December	41.8	48	0.48	0.31	0.2	0.99
Total	262.2	250	2.50	0.53	1.2	4.23

The system is obviously unfair as it gives the salesman making the most sales, remuneration totalling only just half of that obtained by his colleague. Indeed it seems likely that the fluctuations in Simon Smooth's sales have been artificially generated by careful timing of when he records orders obtained. If this is so, then service to customers is being adversely affected by their having to wait longer than necessary in having their orders filled.

The main culprit is the bonus given for exceeding the budget target. This will inevitably encourage salesmen to make an effort to have some very good months, but to make little effort in below average months. This amplification of natural fluctuations is compounded by the way in which the budget target is set. Alternate months, having low sales followed by high sales, yield very high bonuses. This is undesirable and unnecessarily costly. The sales commission, although a commonly used device, may also have undesirable effects by encouraging sales of high value items, but possibly low profit, at the expense of lower value but more profitable items.

It must always be borne in mind that the purpose of a compensation system is to motivate the salesman to act in the company's best interest by acting in his own best interest. Any proposed system must be examined to ensure that it contains no loop-holes by which undesirable behaviour can yield high salaries. The main factors that need to be considered in designing an improved system are :

(a) The relative amount of fixed base salary to variable commission required. Low base salaries may motivate a high sales effort, but possibly at the expense of customer service; high base salaries may not be considered to give adequate motivation for sales effort in a job that is necessarily unsupervised.

(b) The basis on which commission is calculated. Product contribution rather than gross value may produce a more effective sales mix.

(c) Special bonuses, used to stress particular lines at different times, should be periodically set and updated, together with special offers and other promotional devices.

(d) The method of setting sales targets and the period over which a bonus is calculated should be carefully considered.

Further reading: Armstrong, M. and Murlis, H. (1988).

CHAPTER 4

THE MANAGEMENT OF BUSINESS ENTERPRISES

1. It is true that the management control systems framework views all managerial activity as control activity. Decision-making is the implementation of actions designed to achieve objectives; planning is anticipatory or feed-forward control; intelligence gathering is a means of improving predictive models, and so on. The important question is how helpful is it to regard the process of management from this perspective?

There are many specific areas of management that do not significantly benefit from this viewpoint. The details of day-to-day managerial work in most functional specialities, be it production, marketing, personnel, industrial relations or finance, require other, more detailed models to assist the manager to do his job effectively. Yet, nevertheless, the control framework does distil one common and central aspect of all managerial work. That is, it is concerned with the integration of a variety of activities (often involving the work of other managers) into a co-ordinated package designed to achieve certain overall objectives. Thus the control systems framework provides an essential overall perspective without which it is easy not to see the wood for the trees.

Perhaps the one circumstance in which the central framework is not helpful is when there is no clear overall objective for an organization. Activity is fragmented as various groups seek to further their own purposes; overall organizational coherence occurs only by chance. However, in such circumstances it is unlikely that the organization will survive; rather it will tend to disintegrate into new parts.

Reference: Vickers, G. (1967), Chapter 7

Further reading: Lowe, E.A. and J.L.F. Machin (1983), Chapter 2.

2. Since 1960 there has been a great proliferation of quantitative aids to management decision-making, many of them developed under the banner of 'operational research'. They have been concerned with the whole spectrum of managerial activity ranging from problems of operational control (e.g. job-shop scheduling, inventory control, queuing) to overall strategic issues (e.g. corporate planning, portfolio theory). The technique of linear programming in particular has been applied to a wide range of problems (see Chapter 6 for a fuller discussion).

However, managers have generally shown no marked enthusiasm in adopting such techniques, although it is of interest to note that they have probably been used more in the operational area than in the strategic arena. Three main classes of reason have been put forward to explain this general lack of use:

(a) Managers do not understand the quantitative techniques and do not appreciate what they can do.

(b) Quantification of a decision removes the role of managerial discretion and may prevent a manager from taking actions he wishes to take, for reasons other than corporate optimization.

(c) The available techniques capture only part of the complexity of the real world and are not really very helpful in dealing with most major managerial decisions.

Most attention has been directed to the first reason, although the increasing sophistication of managerial education makes it less likely to be true. The third reason undoubtedly has some validity, particularly at senior management levels, but improved models continue to be developed. The second reason is probably the cause

32

of much resistance; managers may not wish to be constrained by being too specific about their objectives. Decisions may be designed to partly satisfy multiple objectives.

Reference: Tomlinson, R. (1981)

Further reading: Scapens, R.W. (1984)

3.   Mintzberg's study involved the work of chief executives and therefore perhaps exaggerates the chaotic aspects of managerial work at lower levels. Nevertheless, many managers at all levels would recognize the problems that Mintzberg outlines. But in all managerial work there is a balance to be maintained between organizing the routine, so that it occurs without fuss, and responding to the unexpected. Routine work can be delegated, subject to regular monitoring that it is being carried out appropriately; the unexpected is more demanding of managerial time. However, it is always the case that the urgent drives out the less urgent, but possibly more important work, as many handbooks on the management of managerial time emphasize. The sections on decentralization and divisionalization in Chapter 2 have considerable relevance to this question.

A senior manager has many competing demands on his time and it is essential that this is organized so that he attends to the most important matters (i.e. those that only he can do). However, we all face similar problems in our everyday life, and it can be instructive to let students answer this question with respect to other academic work and other activities.

Reference: Mintzberg, H. (1973)

Further reading: Mintzberg, H. (1979)

4. There is considerable validity in this statement, although it must be recognized that many non-financial managers can be highly effective without using accounting information. This applies particularly to those able to personally supervise the activities they are responsible for (e.g. when profitability declines due to price reductions elsewhere). In addition, accounting provides a language for the upward transmission of information about overall performance to superiors although the importance of this will vary. For example, in single product industries much information can be transmitted in physical terms whereas in a diversified company accounting information is essential. Thus it is important to distinguish information useful to the manager in controlling his own operations and that transmitted to his boss regarding overall performance. It is also necessary to distinguish between financial information (about money) and information about other matters (e.g. production, marketing) expressed, for convenience, in monetary terms.

Further reading: Hopwood, A.G. (1974); Dew, R.B. and Gee, K.P. (1973)

5. This question is intended to encourage students to apply Mintzberg's recommendations in practical terms, by reference to a small business that is easily understood and which probably has little requirement for much formal information. Nevertheless it still needs information on its customers and potential customers, competitors, suppliers etc.

Reference: Mintzberg, H. (1975)

6. Organizational culture, or the dominant norms and values prevalent in an organization, is a potent form of control. Groups reward members for keeping in line with their shared values and tend to punish deviant behaviour. There is little doubt that some cultures are more appropriate than others for certain tasks, and Handy's

categorization into club, role, task and existential cultures is illuminating. However, cultures can develop that are inappropriate and unhelpful to task performance. This can particularly occur when changes in the external environment requires new ways of performing tasks to be developed; the existing culture can be a powerful inhibitor of change (e.g. bureaucratic cultures stressing the following of rules and regulations when these no longer apply). Other examples would include the attempts to instill a customer service culture into organizations (often monopolies or publicly owned) that previously did not stress this (e.g. British Airways, British Rail).

Reference: Handy (1978) — (3rd edition now available (1985)).

7. This question seeks to place accounting controls in their proper perspective. Although accounting controls are vital to overall control by senior management, company cultures can play as more important part (e.g. contrast the financial accountability controls used by GEC with the different cultures operated by firms a distinct as IBM and Marks and Spencer). At lower organizational levels the impact of accounting controls dwindles and the importance of a wide variety of other controls increases.

Some examples would be peer group control, emphasized by promotion criteria in organisations as disparate as universities (publications in research journals) and coal-mining (man-management skills). Personnel selection procedures have an evident importance, for by importing participants who have been educated in a given way and who may thus start a wide range of common values, much behaviour can be taken for granted rather than explicitly controlled (e.g. City institutions recruiting from public schools).

Reference: Merchant, K. (1985a)

Further reading: Macintosh, N.B. (1985) <u>The Social Software of Accounting</u>
<u>and Information Systems</u>, New York, Wiley.

8.   Senior managers have to be concerned with the overall operations of their enterprise.   Inevitably, being involved in a wider range of matters, and with the relationship of the enterprise to the outside world, makes it difficult for the manager to have a detailed knowledge of what is happening within the organization.   In this sense it is likely to be true that the manager knows less and less about more and more.

Such a state of affairs makes it more necessary than ever that an adequate *system* of management control exists, so that matters that he needs to know about are brought to the manager's attention.   However, although *actual* performance along different dimensions can be reported, it is more difficult for the manager to know what *standard* of performance is appropriate, lacking the necessary detailed knowledge.   To some extent, this task can be delegated to subordinates, but they, too are motivated to be less than totally frank about their own performance standards (see the more extensive discussion on budgeting in Chapter 7).   This is the central problem studied by agency theory (i.e. how to set up a contract to give optimal performance in a situation characterized by information asymmetry) and this perspective can be used to throw light on the design of management control systems.
Reference: Scapens, R.W. (1984) pp. 63-74

9.   One approach to constructing a definition of management control systems is to regard each work as defining a progressively smaller subset of activities. Thus management is a subset of all those things that go on in an organization; control is a subset of all the activities that managers undertake, systems refers to formal,

systematic data-handling systems. This can be tied into Anthony's (1965) definition of management control as 'the process by which managers assure that resources are obtained and used effectively and efficiently in the accomplishment of the organization's objectives'.

However, such a definition carries within it the seeds of several problems. Is management control something that only managers do, or should it involve all organizational participants? Is control the implementation of plans, or should it include the formation and revision of such plans? Does the term 'systems' refer primarily to being 'systematic' or rather to taking a 'systemic' perspective? Should the definition of management control have more to say about the purpose of the system? Is the level of analysis of individual, the organization or society at large? How does management control relate to organizational control?

The objective of this question is not to produce a robust definition, but rather to appreciate the issues that are raised in any attempt to do so. Like management control itself, it is the process rather than the result that is most important.

Reference: Anthony, R.N. (1965)

Further reading: Lowe, E.A. and J.L.J. Machin (1983) — Chapters 2, 3, 4 and 14.

10. Formal information forms part of the world-taken-for-granted by a senior manager. It provides him with background information about what has actually happened, both inside and outside his organization. However, historical information has only a loose relationship with predictive information about what is likely to happen in the future. It is necessary but not sufficient for the process of prediction.

Much of a senior manager's work is concerned with adopting the behaviour of his organization to meet the circumstances that it will face in the future. Typically, the more senior the manager, the longer-term will be his planning horizon (and his time-span of discretion). Thus much of the information he will use to predict the likely turn of future events will be informal, *ad hoc* and uncertain. He will obtain such information in several ways from a variety of sources, but much of it will be based on personal interaction.

Thus the paradox may be mainly apparent. Formal information provides vital background against which other information can, in part, be validated, but rarely provides the driving force behind managerial activity. The manager's life style may be well-suited to the type of information he deals in. However, there is a danger that the style of life described by Mintzberg may encourage a 'fire-fighting' style of management that neglects longer-term planning for immediate intervention. Although this may occasionally be necessary to ensure organizational survival, it is probably not an appropriate style for effective management.

Reference: Dew, R.B. and K.P. Gee (1973)

Further reading: Dermer, J. (1977)

11. The main contrast drawn in the chapter is between rational uses of information and political (or self-interested) uses. Most formal information systems are designed on rational assumptions i.e. how will this information be used to pursue organizational goals? In practice, the use of information will be overlaid with political motivations i.e. how will disclosure or transmission of this information assist me to achieve my objectives? The different analyses are complementary. All action is governed by individual motives; the art of management control is to harness such individual motivation and direct it so that organizational objectives are attained.

Reference: Pettigrew, A. (1973)

Further reading: Willmott, H. (1984)

12. This is a good question! Many studies indicate the lack of reliance often placed on formal information systems, the methods used to circumvent them and the inaccuracies they often contain. Nevertheless, formal information systems provide a cornerstone for effective control. But it must be recognized that although formal systems provide the basis for keeping routine and well-understood activities under control, much managerial work consists of helping the organization to adapt to change and to cope with ambiguity. The formal system may be the bedrock of routine control, but informal systems are needed to cope with uncertainty and the management of change. Whether formal information systems can be designed to do this latter task more effectively is an open question (see further reading).

Reference: Earl, M.J. and Hopwood, A.G. (1981)

Further reading Hedberg, B. and Jonsson, S. (1978)

13. Each sector of the business evidently faces quite different problems and requires quite different methods of coping with them. It is therefore likely that the methods of control and performance evaluation will also have to be different in each part of the business.

The main feature of the market for electronic products is one of rapid change, technological obsolesence and consumer tastes that are unpredictable. Who, for example, could have predicted the market for home computers and games machines when such products were virtually non-existent? The Marketing Manager's main problem is to assess what products are likely to sell in the short-term and to arrange advertising (what media aimed at what potential customers?) and distribution (what channels?) to move appropriate quantities. Pricing is also probably a critical decision for the company, to be taken in close collaboration with the board of directors. The Marketing Manager's critical needs are for up-to-date external market information and the ability to adapt rapidly to market changes.

By contrast the Production Manager requires some protection from these rapid changes. Once a product has been designed he is required to make adequate quantities efficiently and reliably to meet market demands. Frequent design changes and rapidly changing production schedules will impair his ability to produce cheaply. There will always be a compromise to be made between efficient production and speedy adaption. In this kind of company, this must be a top-level decision; once made, for whatever period even if only for a few days, the production process should be insulated from the turbulent environment in the interests of efficiency.

The R and D Manager's problems are of a different nature to the above. He is concerned with utilizing the latest technological advances and developing them so that they can be incorporated into saleable products. This requires both close co-operation with the Marketing Manager in a joint dialogue (both 'this is what we can make, can you sell it?' and 'this is what we can sell, can you make it?'), and taking decisions about what lines of research to pursue in the face of high uncertainty about outcomes. Although there are trade-offs between what is developed, how long it takes and what it will cost, these are very difficult to quantify, and traditional methods of budgeting control inappropriate.

It might be argued that the logical sequence of functional skills in this type of industry is that of R and D then Marketing, then Production. What is produced is primarily determined by the kinds of product that are technically feasible to make, the next consideration is developing a market for this type of product; actually manufacturing it is a consequence of decisions taken in the first two stages. In terms of theoretical approaches, it appears that although a mechanistic view of production might be appropriate Marketing and R and D require a more organic approach. Contingency theories suggest that the different parts of the company require different types of accounting information and control systems. Marketing requires good external information (mainly non-accounting) and access to accounting information that will enable the marketing manager to quickly assess the likely consequences of various pricing policies and the effectiveness of advertising expenditure. R and D might be best managed with program budgets, but with the recognition that large variations from budget are to be expected. Production requires a standard costing system possibly with experience learning factors built-in. The Accountant and Chief Executive both need to realize that different controls are appropriate to different parts of this business, and should avoid trying to impose what works well in one part upon others for which it would be quite inappropriate.

CHAPTER 5

CONTROLS IN BUSINESS ORGANIZATIONS

1. In this chapter control is discussed as if it were separable from objective setting and strategy formulation; it involves taking steps to ensure that the people in the organization implement the chosen strategy. With this meaning, control can be considered as equivalent to strategy implementation.

Keep in mind, however, that some meanings of the word control are broader than the one used here. (This lack of precision was discussed in Chapter 1.) Some people, for example, include efforts to judge whether a strategy is valid (or still valid) under the rubric control. These 'strategic control' efforts are outside the meaning most would attach to the phrase strategy implementation.

2. The questions that should be used to place the control types on the usability continuum are identical to the questions described in the text as leading to the judgements of feasibility. Thus in deciding whether or not action controls are usable, for example, the control system designers must assess both the extent to which knowledge exists about what actions are desirable and the extent to which the desired behaviours can be tracked. The designers must keep in mind that the answers to these questions will sometimes not lead to an absolute yes-no answer as to whether a particular type of control can be used. The design task then becomes one of fitting imperfect solutions together into a system of devices that provides effective control.

3. The purpose of all controls is to influence individuals' behaviours (or actions). In this sense, all controls are action controls. Some controls are just more direct than others.

4. Results controls have one major advantage over action controls, particularly; they allow the people whose behaviours are being controlled a certain freedom of action. People are given the freedom to figure out how best to generate the desired results. This freedom often leads to creative improvements in ways of doing things and higher motivation.

But results controls also have their limitations. In particular, often the results that can be measured are imperfect surrogates of what the organization truly desires. For example, many organizations want profits to be generated over the long-term, but they base their results controls only on short-term profits. Because these measurement imperfections are quite significant in many situations, it is not true that results controls should be used wherever they are feasible.

5. It is important that organizations maintain tight control over the short list of items that can be considered their critical success factors. The challenge is to provide this tight control without having the control system appear as stifling.

What causes control systems to appear as stifling? One common cause is a heavy use of action controls allows employees no autonomy. In such cases, the stifling nature of the controls can be avoided by allowing action autonomy in areas that are not as critical to the organization's success. Another common reason why employees consider control systems as stifling is the basing of results controls on short-term measures that induce actions that the employees know are not in the best long-term interest of the corporation. The solution here is to improve the results measures.

6. Managers must periodically (or continually) ask themselves what it is that their organization must do well to succeed. The answer to this question depends both on the market(s) in which they are competing and their chosen strategy (e.g., cost leadership vs. product differentiation).

Control feasibility can also affect the organization's choice of strategy and thus its critical success factors. For example, if direct sales activities are essential to the proper implementation of the organization's chosen strategy, then the organization must ensure that the controls over its salesforce are effective. If they are not, they must be made effective or the strategy must be altered.

CHAPTER 6

ACCOUNTING FOR DECISION MAKING

1. Outline solution tables are given below. The figures are rounded to the nearest integer, but the program used did not use the rounded figures in the subsequent calculations. Annual totals within about 10 or so of the given figures are likely to be correct. This example has been successfully conducted on a BBC micro-computer (using both Ultracalc and Viewsheet) within available memory, and also using Lotus 1-2-3 on an IBM PC and the FCS-EPS financial planning package on a DEC VAX minicomputer.

(a) and (b) Outline solutions are given in Tables 1, 2 and 3.

(c) <u>Reconciliations</u>

	Case (a)	Case (b)(i)	Case (b)(ii)
Profit	54 290	25 366	12 300
Depreciation	36 000	36 000	36 000
Bank overdraft	56 625	22 470	(42 696)
Funds available	146 915	83 836	5 604
Increase in debtors	74 471	39 660	4 104
Increase ub F.G. inv	44 867	29 315	3 500
Increase in R.M. inv	27 577	14 860	(2 000)
Funds used	146 915	83 835	5 604

(a)	Nov	Dec	Jan	Feb	Mar	Apr	May	Jun	Jul	Aug	Sep	Oct	Nov	Dec	Jan	YEAR
Sales of A	5155	5000	4850	4705	4563	4426	4294	4165	4040	3919	3801	3687	3577	3469	3365	49495
Open stock A		2000	2000	2352	2282	2213	2147	2082	2020	1959	1901	1844	1788	1735	1683	
Closing stock A		2000	2352	2282	2213	2147	2082	2020	1959	1901	1844	1788	1735	1683	1632	
Change in A			352	(71)	(68)	(66)	(64)	(62)	(61)	(59)	(57)	(55)	(54)	(52)	(50)	
Required prod. of A			5202	4634	4495	4360	4229	4102	3979	3860	3744	3632	3523	3417	3315	49178
Sales of B	893	1000	1120	1254	1405	1574	1762	1974	2211	2476	2773	3106	3479	3896	4363	27029
Opening of stock B		1000	1000	1254	1405	1574	1762	1974	2211	2476	2773	3106	3479	3896	4363	
Closing stock B		1000	1254	1405	1574	1962	1974	2211	2476	2773	3106	3479	3896	4363	4887	
Change in B			254	151	169	189	211	237	265	297	333	373	417	468	524	
Required prod. of B			1374	1405	1574	1762	1974	2211	2476	2773	3106	3479	3896	4363	4887	30393
Net Revenue A	50515	49000	47530	46104	44721	43379	42078	40816	39591	38403	37251	36134	35050	33998	32978	485056
Var COGS A	38660	37500	36375	35284	34225	33198	32203	31236	30299	29390	28509	27653	26824	26019	25239	371216
Contribution A	11856	11500	11155	10820	10496	10181	9875	9579	9292	9013	8743	8480	8226	7979	7740	113840
Fixed Fact A			9310	8936	8524	8093	7647	7189	6724	6257	5792	5335	4889	4459		83157
Fixed S&D A			500	500	500	500	500	500	500	500	500	500	500	500	500	6000
Profit A			1345	1384	1472	1588	1729	1890	2068	2256	2450	2645	2837	3020		24683
Net Revenue B	15268	17100	19152	21450	24024	29897	33484	37503	42003	47043	52688	59011	66092	74024	82906	506372
Var COGS B	12946	14500	16240	18189	20371	22816	25554	28620	32055	35901	40210	45035	50439	56492	63271	391922
Contribution B	2321	2600	2912	3261	3653	7081	7931	8882	9948	11142	12479	13976	15653	17532	19636	114450
Fixed Fact B			3690	4064	4476	4907	5353	5811	6376	6743	7208	7665	8111	8541		72843
Fixed S&D B			1000	1000	1000	1000	1000	1000	1000	1000	1000	1000	1000	1000		12000
Profit B			(1778)	(1802)	(1823)	1174	1577	2071	2672	3399	4271	5311	6543	7991		29607
Profit A + B			(433)	(418)	(351)	2762	3306	3961	4740	5655	6722	7957	9379	11011		54290
Cash in A			49742	48250	46803	45398	44036	42715	41434	40191	38985	37816	36681	35581		
Cash in B			15654	17532	19636	21992	25261	30652	34330	38450	43064	48232	54020	60502		
Total cash in			65396	65782	66438	67391	69297	73368	75674	78641	82049	86047	90701	96083		
Cash out - L&VO			21104	19522	19779	20130	20583	21150	21842	22672	23656	24810	26152	27705		
Cash out - Materials			32585	33715	35064	36655	38516	40677	43171	46035	49313	53051	57304	62130		
Cash out - Fixed costs			11500	11500	11500	11500	11500	11500	11500	11500	11500	11500	11500	11500		
Cash out - Selling costs			2985	2979	2984	3000	3028	3069	3125	3197	3287	3396	3528	3683		
Total cash out			68174	67716	69327	71285	73627	76396	79638	83404	87756	92757	98484	105018		
Net cash flow			(2779)	(1934)	(2888)	(3894)	(4330)	(3029)	(3873)	(4764)	(5706)	(6710)	(7783)	(8935)		
Cummulative NCE			(2779)	(4712)	(7601)	(11495)	(15825)	(18854)	(22727)	(27491)	(33197)	(39907)	(47690)	(56625)		

b(i)	Nov	Dec	Jan	Feb	Mar	Apr	May	Jun	Jul	Aug	Sep	Oct	Nov	Dec	Jan	YEAR
Sales of A	5155	5000	4750	4513	4287	4073	3869	3675	3492	3317	3151	2994	2844	2702	2567	43666
Open stock A		2000	2000	2256	2143	2036	1934	1838	1746	1659	1576	1497	1422	1351	1283	
Closing stock A			2256	2143	2036	1934	1838	1746	1659	1576	1497	1422	1351	1283	1219	
Change in A			256	(113)	(107)	(102)	(97)	(92)	(87)	(83)	(79)	(75)	(71)	(68)	(64)	
Required prod. of A			5006	4400	4180	3971	3772	3584	3404	3234	3072	2929	2773	2634	2503	42949
Sales of B	893	1000	1100	1210	1331	1464	1611	1772	1949	2144	2358	2594	2853	3138	3452	25323
Opening of stock B		1000	1000	1210	1331	1464	1611	1772	1949	2144	2358	2594	2853	3138	3452	
Closing stock B			1210	1331	1464	1611	1772	1949	2144	2358	2594	2853	3138	3452	3797	
Change in B			210	121	133	146	161	177	195	214	236	259	285	314	345	
Required prod. of B			1310	1331	1464	1611	1772	1949	2144	2358	2594	2853	3138	3452	3797	25975
Net Revenue A	50515		46550	44223	42011	39911	37915	36020	34219	32508	30882	29338	27871	26478	25154	427925
Var COGS A	38660		35625	33844	32152	30544	29017	27566	26188	24878	23634	22453	21330	20264	19250	327493
Contribution A	11856		10925	10379	9860	9367	8898	8454	8031	7629	7248	6885	6541	6214	5903	100431
Fixed Fact A			9336	8942	8522	8083	7627	7160	6686	6209	5736	5271	4819	4383		82774
Fixed S&D A			500	500	500	500	500	500	500	500	500	500	500	500		6000
Profit A		1089	1089	937	838	784	771	794	845	920	1012	1114	1222	1331		11657
Net Revenue B	15268	17100	18810	20691	22760	27818	30600	33660	37026	40728	44801	49281	54209	59630	65593	440014
Var COGS B	12946	14500	15950	17545	19300	21229	23352	25688	28256	31082	34190	37609	41370	45507	50058	341079
Contribution B	2321	2600	2860	3146	3461	6588	7247	7972	8769	9646	10611	11672	12839	14123	15535	98934
Fixed Fact B			3664	4058	4478	4917	5373	5840	6314	6791	7264	7729	8181	8617		73226
Fixed S&D B			1000	1000	1000	1000	1000	1000	1000	1000	1000	1000	1000	1000		12000
Profit B			(1804)	(1912)	(2017)	671	874	1132	1455	1856	2347	2943	3658	4506		13708
Profit A + B			(715)	(975)	(1180)	1455	1646	1926	2300	2775	3359	4057	4880	5837		25366
Cash in A			49742	47750	45363	43094	40940	38893	36948	35101	33346	31678	30094	28590		
Cash in B			15644	17460	19206	21127	23825	28404	31244	34368	37805	41586	45744	50319		
Total cash in			65396	65210	64569	64221	64765	67296	68192	69469	71151	73264	75839	78908		
Cash out - L&VO			20259	18523	18396	18354	18403	18546	18788	19134	19592	20169	20872	21712		
Cash out - Materials			30909	31360	31988	32804	33821	35053	36516	38227	40207	42476	45060	47985		
Cash out - Fixed costs			11500	11500	11500	11500	11500	11500	11500	11500	11500	11500	11500	11500		
Cash out - Selling costs			2925	2861	2809	2768	2740	2724	2720	2730	2755	2794	2849	2920		
Total cash out			65593	64244	64692	65427	66464	67823	69254	71592	74054	76939	80281	84117		
Net cash flow			(197)	966	(124)	(1206)	(1699)	(526)	(1332)	(2123)	(2903)	(3675)	(4442)	(5209)		
Cumulative NCE			(197)	769	645	(561)	(2260)	(2786)	(4118)	(6241)	(9144)	(12819)	(17261)	(22470)		

TABLE 3

b(ii)

	Nov	Dec	Jan	Feb	Mar	Apr	May	Jun	Jul	Aug	Sep	Oct	Nov	Dec	Jan	YEAR
Sales of A	5155	5000	5000	5000	5000	5000	5000	5000	5000	5000	5000	5000	5000	5000	5000	60000
Open stock A		2000	2000	2500	2500	2500	2500	2500	2500	2500	2500	2500	2500	2500	2500	
Closing stock A			2500	2500	2500	2500	2500	2500	2500	2500	2500	2500	2500	2500	2500	
Change in A		500	500	0	0	0	0	0	0	0	0	0	0	0	0	
Required prod. of A			5500	5000	5000	5000	5000	5000	5000	5000	5000	5000	5000	5000	5000	60500
Sales of B	893	1000	1000	1000	1000	1000	1000	1000	1000	1000	1000	1000	1000	1000	1000	12000
Opening of stock B		1000	1000	1000	1000	1000	1000	1000	1000	1000	1000	1000	1000	1000	1000	
Closing stock B			1000	1000	1000	1000	1000	1000	1000	1000	1000	1000	1000	1000	1000	
Change in B			0	0	0	0	0	0	0	0	0	0	0	0	0	
Required prod. of B			1000	1000	1000	1000	1000	1000	1000	1000	1000	1000	1000	1000	1000	12000
Net Revenue A	50515	49000	49000	49000	49000	49000	49000	49000	49000	49000	49000	49000	49000	49000	49000	588000
Var COGS A	38660	37500	37500	37500	37500	37500	37500	37500	37500	37500	37500	37500	37500	37500	37500	450000
Contribution A	11856	11500	11500	11500	11500	11500	11500	11500	11500	11500	11500	11500	11500	11500	11500	138000
Fixed Fact A			10214	10000	10000	10000	10000	10000	10000	10000	10000	10000	10000	10000	10000	120214
Fixed S&D A			500	500	500	500	500	500	500	500	500	500	500	500	500	6000
Profit A			786	1000	1000	1000	1000	1000	1000	1000	1000	1000	1000	1000	1000	11786
Net Revenue B	15268	17100	17100	17100	17100	19000	19000	19000	19000	19000	19000	19000	19000	19000	19000	222300
Var COGS B	12946	14500	14500	14500	14500	14500	14500	14500	14500	14500	14500	14500	14500	14500	14500	174000
Contribution B	2321	2600	2600	2600	2600	4500	4500	4500	4500	4500	4500	4500	4500	4500	4500	48300
Fixed Fact B			2786	3000	3000	3000	3000	3000	3000	3000	3000	3000	3000	3000	3000	35786
Fixed S&D B			1000	1000	1000	1000	1000	1000	1000	1000	1000	1000	1000	1000	1000	12000
Profit B			(1186)	(1400)	(1400)	500	500	500	500	500	500	500	500	500	500	514
Profit A + B			(400)	(400)	(400)	1500	1500	1500	1500	1500	1500	1500	1500	1500	1500	12300
Cash in A			49742	49000	49000	49000	49000	49000	49000	49000	49000	49000	49000	49000	49000	
Cash in B			15654	17100	17100	17100	17500	19000	19000	19000	19000	19000	19000	19000	19000	
Total cash in			65396	66100	66100	66100	66500	68000	68000	68000	68000	68000	68000	68000	68000	
Cash out - L&VO			20500	19000	19000	19000	19000	19000	19000	19000	19000	19000	19000	19000	19000	
Cash out - Materials			30000	30000	30000	30000	30000	30000	30000	30000	30000	30000	30000	30000	30000	
Cash out - Fixed costs			11500	11500	11500	11500	11500	11500	11500	11500	11500	11500	11500	11500	11500	
Cash out - Selling costs			3000	3000	3000	3000	3000	3000	3000	3000	3000	3000	3000	3000	3000	
Total cash out			65000	63500	63500	63500	63500	63500	63500	63500	63500	63500	63500	63500	63500	
Net cash flow			396	2600	2600	2600	3000	4500	4500	4500	4500	4500	4500	4500	4500	
Cummulative NCE			396	2996	5596	8196	11196	15696	20196	24696	29196	33696	38196	42696		

Evidently, the best profit figures are associated with the largest cash flows and thus the greatest bank overdraft. Extra financing is needed if the projections in all cases are to be realizable.

(d) These two objectives conflict directly. Maximum profit is achieved only at the expense of poor cash flow. Although much could be done to reduce cash outflows, particularly in terms of reducing payment periods and bad debts for product B, this might well affect sales. It is possible the Manageing Director may choose a less profitable strategy (for who knows what profit might have been?) that keeps cash reserves constant, rather than a policy such as case (a). The overdraft is clearly observable; the profit that might have been obtained is not.

Further reading: Sherwood, D. (1983)

2.   The following formulation allows production of A_2 to be limited to 600 units, and also allows an amount A_{2S} of A_2 to be sold on the external market (although not bought in from it). By setting the proceeds of such a sale to zero, the first part of the question can be solved and then by changing these proceeds to £3, £6, and £9 the additional questions can be answered.

a_1	a_2	b_1	b_2	a_{2s}		
1	2				$\leq$	2000
3	1				$\leq$	2000
		1	1		$\leq$	300
		1	2		$\leq$	400
-1		2	1		$\leq$	0
	-1	3	2	1	$\leq$	0
	1				$\leq$	600

Maximize   -4   -3   24   20 0^*

a_{2s} is the quantity of A_2 sold on the external market

* price obtained from selling A_2 on external market

With the new constraint limiting production of A_2 to 600 units, the total contribution is reduced to £2,200. 350 units of A_1 and 600 units of A_2 are produced and converted into 100 units of B_1 and 150 units of B_2. Constraint 4 is binding and has a shadow price of £4 per machine hour; also constraint 7 has a shadow price of £1 indicating that A_2 is valued at (£3 + £1 =) £4 per unit. Thus the transfer price should be £4 per unit for both A_1 and A_2, and the Alpha Division will therefore be allocated a contribution of £600 and the Beta Division £1600.

(a) If A_2 can be sold at £3, this is less than its value within the firm (£4) and the optimal solution does not change.

(b) If the external selling price of A_2 now rises to £6 it is worthwhile to sell 200 units of it on the external market at this price. Internally 200 units of A_1 and 400 units of A_2 are converted into 200 units of B_2. Constraint 4 is still binding, but now has a shadow price of only £2, constraint 7 has a shadow price of £3 reflecting the value (£3 + £3) of A_2 on the external market. Thus the internal transfer prices should be £4 for A_1 and £6 for A_2. The total contribution of £2 600 will be split £1 800 to the Alpha Division and £800 to the Beta Division.

(c) When the external price for A_2 increases to £9, it it not worthwhile to process it further internally. Thus the contribution of (600 units x £6) = £3,600 accrues totally to the Alpha Division, the Beta Division does no work and receives no contribution.

Reference: Whitaker, D. O.R. on the Micro, Wiley, 1984. Contains a useful computer program for solving small L.P. problems.

Further reading: Mepham, M.J. (1980)

3. (a) Schedule for B's profit at various levels of sales

Sales (units)	Revenue £	Costs B's costs	Costs Transferred by A	Costs Total	B's profit
1000	1750	1250	400	1650	100
2000	2650	1500	800	2300	350
3000	3300	1750	1200	2950	350
4000	3700	2000	1600	3600	100
5000	4000	2250	2000	4250	(250)
6000	4000	2500	2400	4900	(900)

(b) B is indifferent between sales of 2 000 units and sales of 3 000 units as both yield B a profit of £350 per day. A will therefore make a smaller profit than it might, and the company is certainly not optimizing, as shown below:

(c)

Sales (units)	Revenue £	Costs B'costs	A's costs	Total	Company profit
1000	1750	1250	550	1800	(50)
2000	2650	1500	650	2150	500
3000	3300	1750	750	2500	800
4000	3700	2000	850	2850	850
5000	4000	2250	950	3200	800
6000	4000	2500	1050	3550	450

(d)

Sales (units)	A's profit	B's profit	Total profit
1000	(150)	100	(50)
2000	150	350	500
3000	450	350	800
4000	750	100	850
5000	1050	(250)	800
6000	1350	(900)	450

The reason for B selecting a sub-optimal level of output lies in the high transfer price charged by A. The corporate optimum occurs at sales of 4 000 units, but B makes less profit here than at a lower level of sales. If the transfer price were lowered to (say) 20p per unit, then B would have an incentive to sell more, but still only up to 3000 units. Note however that A makes a loss of £150 at this price and level of output, compared to a profit of £150 (or £450, depending upon B's choice of output level) when 40p is charged.

Corporate optimality is only obtained when the transfer price is reduced to the variable cost of production. B is now motivated to select the optimal level of output for the company, but A makes a loss equal to its fixed costs i.e. £550.

Reference: See Chapter 11 for a fuller discussion

Further reading: Tomkins, C. (1973)

4.   (a) The contribution analysis indicates a steadily rising total contribution to profit as price drops with a fairly flat peak in the range £28 to £40. However, once price drops below £28 total contribution falls rapidly to zero at a price of £16. Because of possible estimation errors it would therefore appear wise to set the target price for mass sales at about £40. Nevertheless the very marked changes in demand with price suggest that greater returns might be obtained by exploiting the fact that a small number of customers would appear to be willing to pay a high price for the product, a state of affairs that will be most pronounced when the product is introduced. Thus a possible pricing policy which would give a high contribution would be to attempt the following:

Stage	Description	Contribution
1	High price of £128 for initial introduction. Demand is 1 000 units over 2 year period, say 400 in introductory period.	
		44 800
2	Price reduction to £64 for remainder of first year. Demand = 4 000 over 2 years, say 2 400 in first year, of which 400 sold at a higher price = 2 000.	
		96 000
3	Price reduced to £40. Demand = 10 250, over 2 years, say 6 000 in shorter period less 2 400 sold = 3,600.	
		86 400
4	Price reduced to £24. Demand = 28 000 over 2 years say 18 000 in shorter period less 6 000 sold = 12 000	
		96 000
5	Price reduced to £20. Demand = 41 000 over 2 years, say 30 000 in shorter period less 18 000 sold = 12 000.	
		48 000
	Total contribution	£371 200

The estimates of demand in the above analysis may well be optimistic as they need to assume the speed at which demand at a particular price will occur. Although ideally the price would be held until the expected sales were achieved, in practice this might well be undercut by competitors and force an earlier reduction. Further if there is over-capacity at a given price there is a great temptation to reduce prices to gain access to a much increased market; however once price drops below £32 this quickly becomes counter-productive and firms will be forced to withdraw from the market (as occurred in the electronic calculator market in the late 1970s).

A further limitation on this strategy is that purchasers may anticipate price reductions and delay purchasing the product until the price falls. Thus too frequent price changes are likely to be counter productive, and a better policy might be to restrict price changes to just three giving a similar overall result:

Stage		Description	Contribution
1	Introduction	Price below competition for a better product say £64. Demand = 4 000 units – 2 000 = 2 000 over a short period.	
			96 000
2	Mass market	Major price reduction after introductory period to £32. Demand = 16 000 – 2 000 = 14 000 over main life span.	
			224 000
3	Clearance	Final price to gain contribution from low price £20. Demand = 41 000 – 16 000 = 25 000 max. but dependent on competitive situation, say 12 500.	
			50 000
			370 000

55

(b) Price is only one component of the marketing mix. Other suggested components are product, place and promotion. Here the company has developed what it believes to be a superior product, although it is likely that this will be only short-lived and that the product will be quite obsolete in just two years. In order to gain the substantial contribution from those willing to pay a high price for a new product, it is important that such sales are made quickly. There is thus a case for intensive promotion to capture those customers. With such a small number of potential purchasers highly selective marketing is desirable via such devices as specialist chess magazines etc. As the market is likely to be geographically dispersed, mail order sales may be more appropriate than sales via (electronic?) retail shops. Indeeed it may be worth paying substantial sums in market research to discover who buys such games and why. A one-shot advertisement in a Sunday colour supplement would also be a possibility.

Once price is reduced, and a larger market is to be tapped, the appropriate marketing mix is likely to change. The product is being sold more on price; larger numbers of customers must be attracted and other outlets become desirable. Finally, in the clearance stage it may be desirable to allow the discount to be given by retailers, rather than by a change in recommended price, so as to preserve a price structure for future products.

Further reading: Arnold, J. (1973)

5. **Megacorp plc**

(a) Linear program to maximize total contribution of the Megacorp group:

Let L = number of Lemons produced

M = number of Mavericks produced

Maximize 10L + 10M

subject to:

Forging	$9L + 18M <$	810
Grinding	$11L + 10M <$	605
Heating	$10L + 12M <$	630
Rolling	$4L + M <$	160
Stirring	$L + 4M <$	160
Turning	$2L + M <$	90
	$L, M >$	0

Workings

1. Contribution per unit

		L	M
		£	£
Variable costs:			
Ingots	@ £8	8	24
Jars	@ £5	10	10
Knuts	@ £6	<u>12</u>	<u>6</u>
		30	40
Rolling		4	1
Stirring		1	4
Turning		<u>2</u>	<u>1</u>
		37	46
Selling price		<u>47</u>	<u>56</u>
		<u>10</u>	<u>10</u>

2. Hours required in Aira division

	Forging	Grinding	Heating
Lemon:			
Ingots	5	1	2
Jars	2	4	4
Knuts	2	6	4
	9	11	10
Maverick:			
Ingots	15	3	6
Jars	2	4	4
Knuts	1	3	2
	18	10	12

(b) (i) Transfer prices may be calculated as marginal cost to Aira + opportunity cost of scarce resources.

	I	J	K
	£	£	£
Marginal cost	8.000	5.000	6.000
Opportunity Costs:			
Forging	-	-	-
Grinding (62.5 p/hr)	0.625	1.25	1.875
Heating (31.25 p/hr)	0.625	0.625	0.625
	9.25	6.875	8.500

(ii) Contribution for each division

	Aira		Blackside
	£		£
Sales			
- Lemons (30 x £40)	1 200	(30 x £47)	1 410
- Mavericks (27.5 x £50)	1 375	(27.5 x £56)	1 540
Variable costs			
- from Aira			
- Production of:			
I (112.5 x £8)	(900)		-
J (115 x £5)	(575)		-
K (87.5 x £6)	(525)		-
L (30 x £7)	-		(210)
M (27.5 x £6)	-----		(165)
	575		Nil

(c) If the limiting constraints were in the Blackside division rather than the Aira division, the opportunity cost of Aira divisions resources would be nil. The transfer prices would thus be set at just variable cost of the three products. Thus, Aira division would make no contribution (as variable costs would exactly equal revenue) and it would all go to the Blackside division, i.e. the reverse situation to that existing at present.

(d) At present Aira division does not sell ingots, jars and knuts externally. In implementing a market price based system of transfer pricing Megacorp plc would, therefore, immediately face the problem that there is no established market price at present. It would not be an easy task to establish a market price which is realistic without actually entering the external market to allow the forces of supply and demand to operate leading to an equilibrium price. If ingots, jars and knuts are sold externally by other companies then Megacorp plc may take their prices as guidelines.

Aira division is likely to want a higher 'market price' than Blackside division as this will improve its divisional performance. Thus in arriving at a market based transfer price, Aira division will be trying to agree a higher price than is perhaps realistic.

If a realistic market-based transfer price could be agreed upon, then it would allow each division to remain autonomous so that the profit of each division would not be affected by any decision to buy/sell externally or to trade internally. Thus the transfer price shouldn't lead to any divergence between divisional and company goals.

The LP system is essentially a centralized solution; the market-based system (if it is feasible) offers the opportunity of substantial decentralisation.

6. **Argent Company**

   (a) Budgeted profit and loss account

   1 August – 31 October 1988

	£	£
Sales (5 200 units x £25)		130 000
Cost of sales		
Opening stock (2 500 units)	35 300	
Costs of production (5 700 units) (W1)	90 600	
	125 900	
Closing stock (3 000 units) (W2)	46 061	

/Cont....

	£	£
		79 839
Gross profit		50 161
Sales commission (5 200 x 2)	10 400	
Fixed selling & admin costs	18 000	
Bad debts (2% x 130 000)	2 600	
		31 000
Under absorbed fixed overhead		1 350
		⎯⎯⎯
Net profit		17 811

Workings

1. Production costs

	Aug	Sept	Oct	Total	Nov
Sales	1 500	1 800	1 900	5 200	2 000
Opening Stock	(2 500)	(2 700)	(2 850)	(2 500)	(3 000)
Closing stock	2 700	2 850	3 000	3 000	3 750
Production	1 700	1 950	2 050	5 700	2 750

			£
Costs:	Materials	5 700 x £4	22 800
	Labour	5 700 x £5	28 500
	Overtime	50 x £5	250
	Variable overheads	5 700 x £2	11 400
	Lease rental (October only)		2 000
	Absorbed fixed		
	overhead	5 700 x £27 000	25 650
		6 000	90 600

61

2. Closing stock valuation

$$\frac{£125,900}{8\ 200} \times 3,000 = \underline{£46,061}$$

3. Under absorbed fixed overhead

£27 000 - £25 650 $= \underline{£\ 1\ 350}$

(b)

	Aug	Sept	Oct	Total
Receipts				
Sales - July	21 450			21,450
- Aug	7 500	29 250		36,750
- Sept		9 000	35 100	44,100
- Oct			9 500	9,500
	28 950	38 250	44 600	111,800
Payments				
Lease rental			2 000	2,000
Fixed overheads	5 000	5 000	5 000	15,000
Variable overheads	3 400	3 900	4 100	11,400
Sales commission	2 200	3 000	3 600	8,800
Fixed selling costs	6 000	6 000	6 000	18,000
Labour costs	8 500	9 750	10 500	28,750
Materials	6 800	7 800	8 200	22,800
	31 900	35 450	39 400	106,750
Net	(2 950)	2 800	5 200	5,050

Workings

1. **Materials purchases**

	Aug	Sept	Oct	July
	£	£	£	£
Opening stock (units)	1 700	1 950	2 050	
Closing stock	1 950	2 050	2 750	
Increase	250	100	700	
Production	1 700	1 950	2 050	
Purchases	1 950	2 050	2 750	1 700
@ £4	7 800	8 200	11 000	6 800

Reconciliation of profit and cash forecasts

	£
Net profit	17 811

Adjustments for items not involving the

Movement of cash:

Depreciation	12 000
	29 811

Increase(decrease) in working capital

Stock of finished goods	10 761
Stock of raw materials	4 200
Debtors	15 600
Creditors - materials	(4 200)
sales commissions	(1 600)
	(24 761)
Increase in cash	5 050

63

(c) To: Managing director

From: Management accountant

Subject: Overtime working

The purpose of this report is to outline the likely impact of overtime working on profits and the business generally, and to suggest alternative operating strategies.

Impact of overtime working

The existing capacity of the factory is 2 000 units per month. In October and November (and possibly thereafter) this is not adequate. A machine could be leased for £2 000 per month, and overtime worked at double the normal rate, and the capacity could thus be increased to 2 500 units per month.

This proposal will be inefficient for the company because the lease payment and overtime premiums are both very high and unit revenue is not affected by the increased output. Contribution is thus eroded, yet fixed costs are increased.

For the business generally, the overtime may not be a good idea. Employees may not be prepared to work overtime just in those months when the company requires it and, in addition, for a small amount of time (50 units in November). Also as the overtime premium is so great, employees may begin to work slower during normal hours so that overtime working is increased at a great cost to the company.

From the pattern of sales for July to December 1988 it would appear that a steady increase in production is going to be required. Although overtime working may be a satisfactory solution in the short-run in the long-term it

64

almost definitely is not. If the trend in sales and production is likely to continue then overtime working as well as being expensive may not even be able to satisfy the demand.

Alternative strategies

In August and September, the company is not producing to full capacity. The company could consider producing more units in these months to alleviate the problem of paying overtime and leasing the extra machine in later months. However, this is partly a result of the short-term planning horizon currently being used. Problems of the type could be anticipated if budgets were prepared for periods of six months or one year.

Alternatively, the company could revise its stock-holding policy. If less than 150% of the next month's sales was held as stock, then production could be reduced to a certain extent.

A final suggestion would be to use outworkers or part-time workers for production of the product in times when factory capacity is inadequate, or the product could be bought in from a competitor for resale.

These suggestions would need to be appraised to ascertain their effect on profit and cash flow.

7. This problem is missing a necessary item of information, namely the inventory policy for finished goods. It was intended to state that FG inventory at the beginning of each month should equal 50% of expected sales in that month. An alternative solution is given assuming constant inventories.

(a) and (b)

	January	February	March	April
Sales (units)	900	1800	1200	600
FG inv (opening)	200	900	600	300
FG inv (closing)	900	600	300	
Change in FG inv	700	(300)	(300)	
Production required	1600	1500	900	
COG produced				
- Direct labour	2400	2250	1350	
- Direct materials	4400	4125	2475	
- Variable o/h	1200	1125	675	
- Fixed prod costs	8000	8000	8000	
Total prod costs	16 000	15 500	12 500	
Inventory valuation				
FG opening	2000	9000	6125	3725
Prod cost	16 000	15 500	12 500	
Total value	18 000	24 500	18 625	
COGS	9000	18 375	14 900	
FG closing	9000	6125	3725	
Profit and loss				
Sales revenue	10 800	21 600	14 400	
COGS	(9000)	(18 375)	(14 900)	
S & A	(1500)	(1500)	(1500)	
Net profit	300	1725	(2000)	
Cash flows				
Cash in (1 month)	0	4320	8640	
Cash in (2 month)	0	0	6480	
Cash out	(14 500)	(14 000)	(11 000)	
Net cash flow	(14 500)	(9680)	(4120)	

(a) and (b) - alternative solutions

	January	February	March	April
Sales (units)	900	1800	1200	600
FG inv (opening)	200	200	200	200
FG inv (closing)	200	200	200	
Change in FG inv	0	0	0	
Production required	900	1800	1200	
COG produced				
- Direct labour	1350	2700	1800	
- Direct materials	2475	4950	3300	
- Variable o/h	675	1350	900	
- Fixed prod costs	8000	8000	8000	
Total prod costs	12 500	17 000	14 000	
Inventory valuation				
FG opening	2000	2636	1964	2281
Prod cost	12 500	17 000	14 000	
Total value	14 500	19 636	15 964	
COGS	11 864	17 673	13 683	
FG closing	2 636	1 964	2 281	
Profit and loss				
Sales revenue	10 800	21 600	14 400	
COGS	(11 864)	(17 673)	(13 683)	
S & A	(1 500)	(1 500)	(1 500)	
Net profit	(2 564)	2 427	(783)	
Cash flows				
Cash in (1 month)	0	4320	8640	
Cash in (2 month)	0	0	6480	
Cash out	(11 000)	(15 500)	(12 500)	
Net cash flow	(11 000)	(11 180)	2 620	

(c) Profit is driven by changes in production as well as by sales, because fixed costs are included in inventory valuations. For March

	Original	**Alternative**
Profit	(2000)	(783)
Depreciation	3000	3000
Reduction in FG	2400	(317)
Reduction in creditors	720	720
Cash Flow	4120	2620
	====	====

8. **Caradoc Company**

(a + b)

The L.P. formulation is given below. If the products A1 to A3 cannot be sold on an external market, then the columns relating to A1E, A2E and A3E can be omitted or, more simply, the prices P1, P2 and P3 set to zero.

A1, A2, A3   quantities produced of each intermediate product

A1E, A2E, A3E quantities sold on external market

B1, B2   quantities sold of each final product

P1, P2, P3   market prices for intermediate product

For B1 contribution =   £50−£7 =   £43

B2   =   £60−£9 =   £51

	A1	A2	A3	A1E	A2E	A3E	B1	B2		
Machine L	1	2	1						<	480
" M	1	3	2						<	715
" N	1	2	3						<	680
Production of A1	-1			1			3	1	<	0
" " A2		-1			1		2	2	<	0
" " A3			-1			1	1	3	<	0
Machine X							5	3	<	270
" Y							4	6	<	300
Objective function	-4	-7	-9	P1	P2	P3	43	51		

(n.b.   There are two errors in the question as printed in early editions in that the availability of machine M should be 680 hours, not 640 hours. This would affect the optimum solution, which is not feasible as printed. The second error is that the binding constraint in Division B is machine X not machine Y).

(c) Machine L is limiting resource in division A. The transfer price for each intermediate product should be the variable cost of its production plus the shadow price for its usage of machine L.

Product A1 = £4 + 1 hr @ £0.375 = £3.375

" A2 = £7 + 2 hrs @ £0.375 = £7.75

" A3 = £9 + 1 hr @ £0.375 = £9.375

The most straight forward way of calculating the profit for each division is to note that a division is only rewarded for its scarce resources.

Division	A	480 hours of L @	£0.375	=	£180
Division	b	270 hours of X @	£1.00	=	270
		Total profit			£450

Check

Profit of B1 = £50 -   £7 -   3. £4   -   2. £7   - 1. £9

$\quad\quad\quad$ = £43 - £12 - £14   -   £9   = £8

Profit of B2 = £60 -   £9 -   1. £4   -   2. £7   - 3. £9

$\quad\quad\quad$ = £51 -   £4 - £14   -   £27   = £6

Total profit @ optimum =   45 x £8 x   £15 x £6

$\quad\quad\quad\quad\quad\quad$ =   £360   x   £90 =   £450

9. Accounting models are generally static, in the sense that the state of the world is assumed to be fixed and unaffected by the decisions taken by the firm. Thus, if model parameters can be accurately estimated (e.g. variable costs, capacity constraints, demand curves) then the model will produce an optimal solution. Unfortunately these assumptions are not usually valid; external (and internal) conditions are continually changing, and thus the model requires constant up-dating. More seriously, the actions of one firm can affect the decisions taken by other firms, and these consequences ought to be taken into account (e.g. when a petrol company decides on a price change, the reaction of competitors must be predicted).

It may be possible to construct multi-period models that include the effects of such changes, but it is rarely done in practice. What is perhaps more important is to use the restricted accounting model in a more flexible manner, that takes account of its imperfections and limitations. Simple C-V-P analysis can give an insight into basic relationships, but costs change over time. It may be possible to model such changes in cost (e.g. learning curves) and to construct demand curves to produce a

70

more sophisticated model, but even such a model will have its limitations. It is vital to recognize these, and to conduct additional analysis in areas that the crude model indicates are sensitive to the assumptions being made.

Reference: Mepham, M.J. (1980)

Further reading: Kaplan, R.S. and Atkinson, A.A. (1989)

10. General purpose accounting data is prepared by making a large number of assumptions about the stability of relationships and their continuing to hold over a period of time (e.g. a depreciation charge assumes a useful asset life of a number of years; a stock value assumes the good stock will eventually be sold at a normal, or near normal price). Other accounting data makes further assumptions. For example, in the construction of a variable costing statement, relationships between cost and volume are assumed to hold, although they are valid only under certain quite restrictive conditions. Thus, such data can only be validly used in decisions where these assumptions hold.

In a very real sense, there is no such thing as general-purpose accounting data, that is suitable for taking a wide variety of decisions. It invariably needs amending to take account of particular circumstances. For example, Thomas shows that there is no method of cost allocation that is 'harmless' for all decisions, although some methods are harmless for some decisions. His conclusion is that cost allocation should not be included in the production of cost data that will be used for a variety of purposes.

The problem can only be overcome by educating users to be aware of such limitations. When accounting information is used for purposes other than that for which it was originally constructed, great care must be taken to ensure that is adapted in appropriate ways. The example of senior managers scanning a column of product profit figures, and taking action to remove apparent loss-makers is still too common to permit the accountant to assume that users are as aware of accounting data's limitations as they should be.

Reference: Amey, L.R. and Egginton, D. (1973)

Further reading: Thomas, A.L. (1980b)

11. The two major distinguishing features of service industries are that they tend to be labour-intensive and to market a product that is highly perishable. Despite a wide range of differences between service industries which are probably even greater than differences between manufacturing industries, these two characteristics stand out. For example, if one considers the hotel industry, the airline industry and the provision of accounting services as an industry, all are quite heavily labour-intensive. Hotels employ large numbers of staff in a variety of functions to unobtrusively meet the need of their guests; the major expense of professional firms is that of staff costs, and even airlines, that have a heavy investment in capital equipment also have high staff costs. Thus information that aids in the effective management of people is a prime necessity, and it is likely that ideas of responsibility accounting and effective time-management will be of paramount importance. Similarly, each of the industries mentioned has a perishable product; an empty hotel room or an unoccupied aircraft seat represent a revenue-earning opportunity that is gone for ever. Equally, a wasted afternoon for an employee in a professional firm represents an irreplaceable earning opportunity. In all these industries, it is not possible to produce output for stock that can be stored until a customer is willing to buy; real-time considerations dominate.

However, in the private sector at least, the general accounting information provided is not likely to differ in kind; rather it will be the stress that is placed on different kinds of information that will differ. In service industries there is often a need for speedy real-time information. For example, the hotel receptionist and airline booking clerk require up-to-the-minute booking information so as to be in a position to offer appropriate rate discounts for last minute clients. Similarly, the inability to stock products places a premium on staff flexibility to work on different tasks at short notice. The utilization of staff time is of paramount importance in a professional firm, in which one is likely to see control devices, such as time-utilization sheets. As these examples show the fundamental differences between the two types of industry they tend to show up most at the operational level. Once the levels of management and strategic control are reached the differences tend to be minimized. As accounting information is of most use at these higher levels of control, differences in accounting information systems are also likely to be small.

12. A working financial planning model requires data of two kinds. Firstly, it requires the functional form of various relationships to be known (e.g. the relationship of costs to volume of production; the way in which demand will vary with price). Secondly, it requires the parameters for such functional relationships to be estimated (e.g. if costs vary linearly with volume, at what rate?; if price is increased by $x\%$, how much will demand reduce?). Most financial planning texts deal with the former issues at some length, but tend to neglect the latter.

It is probably not sensible to apportion relative importance to each kind of data; both are necessary, However, there is an insidious temptation to use simple functional forms of relationships that can be easily handled by a mathematical model, and then to use the statistical functions built into most financial planning packages to estimate parameter values from past data. The results of such an analysis can give a good indication of the validity of the assessed relationship, at least over past periods (via the variance associated with parameter estimates) but is is easy to overlook this information. It is all too easy to assume a linear relationship, use linear regression to fit parameters, and plug the resultant figures into a model as if they represented absolute truth.

Further reading: Sherwood, D. (1983)

CHAPTER 7

BUDGETARY PLANNING AND CONTROL

1. There are two basic reasons for budget bias. Firstly, a manager may submit a pessimistic budget estimate that will be relatively easy to attain so as to ensure that he achieves his budget target at the end of the period. If performance is evaluated in comparison with the budget, there is an evident motivation to set a budget that will be easy to attain. Secondly, a manager may set an optimistic budget target in order to impress his superior about how well he is going to perform in the future, even though he does not expect actually to attain it. This is evidently not a good long-term strategy, but in some circumstances current, short-term survival may dominate longer-term considerations. There is also the hope that events over the budget period may turn out better than expected. Further pressure for over-optimistic budget estimates may come from senior management who wish to budget for acceptable levels of profit, or to show a year-on-year trend of improvement.

Although senior managers can detect flagrant bias in estimates, they are usually reliant on their subordinates for detailed information on operations. It is therefore unlikely that all bias can be detected and removed by senior managers. Even if it is detected, there may be a case for not formally removing it; a manager may be better motivated by an (admittedly inaccurate) budget he has set himself than by an accurate budget imposed upon him from above. The use of informal 'black-book' budgets by senior managers may stem from this conflict between the best budgets for planning and the best budgets for motivation.

Reference: Lowe, E.A. and Shaw, R.W. (1968)

Further reading: Birnberg, J.G. et al (1983)

2. Modern methods of statistical forecasting can be used to detect trends in time-series or historic information. On the assumption that the underlying situation is stable, then such models may be used to predict further outcomes. There is little doubt that use of such models can reduce the area of discretion open to the subordinate manager, but it is unlikely to remove it completely. Circumstances do change, and new factors come into play. The person in the best position to predict the effect of such changes is usually the manager for whom the budget is being set. It therefore seems unlikely that such techniques will eliminate the problem of budget bias.

Reference: Otley, D.T. (1977), Chapters 4-6.

Further reading: Pfeffer, J. (1981)

3. Work measurement and the derivation of standard costs are quite fundamental to effective systems of budgetary control. Although budgets can be set solely on the basis of past trends, it is vital to relate costs to measures of work actually performed if these are to be used for performance evaluation and responsibility accounting.

Standard costs are the building bricks from which overall budgets are constructed. Once output levels have been planned, it is necessary to estimate the work necessary to achieve such output targets, and its costs. Although this can be done on an ad hoc basis, it is both more accurate and more efficient to do it as a matter of routine. This is the process of standard costing i.e. the setting of carefully pre-determined costs, usually based on work measurement, of performing a task at a given level of efficiency. Of course, the process is not foolproof. As in any budget-setting process, there are motivations for subordinates to inflate the amount of work necessary to achieve a given task, but properly administered such methods are basic to effective budgetary control.

There is a fundamental conflict between the use of budgets for planning purposes, where an accurate forecast is required and their use in control, where the target that will motivate the best effort is required. It is essentially unreasonable to expect both purposes to be served; budgets for one purpose cannot generally be used without modification for the other.

Reference: Yetton, P.W. (1976)

Further reading: Houck, L.D. <u>A Practical Guide to Budgeting and Management Control Systems</u>, Lexington (1979)

4.   The first vital element in effective budgetary control is for the budget standard to be set at an appropriate level. In the context of a profit budget, this implies both the ability to forecast sales at a range of alternative prices (i.e. a demand model) and also knowledge of what must be done in order to produce the goods that will be sold (i.e. knowledge of means–end relationships). Although the attainment of such knowledge is aided by analysis of past trends and comparison with similar units in other places, such trends and comparisons are generally insufficient to arrive at definitive budget standards. The second vital element is the collection of actual data, its comparison with the budget standards and the investigation of corrective action. The first two steps are straightforward (if complex) but the final step requires the determination of the causes of deviations and the generation of apt courses of corrective action (see the control model developed in Chapter 1). Further, more detailed information is required if it is desired to break down components of performance that are the responsibility of individual managers within the overall profit centre.

Thus, very well developed predictive models of all aspects of the production and sales process are required for effective budgetary control to operate. However, if such models exist (i.e. the cause and effect relationships are well-understood), then budgetary control may be unnecessary, as inappropriate performance can be detected and corrected without the need for carefully articulated budget statements expressed in financial terms. An initial financial evaluation, followed by the monitoring of plans to ensure they are implemented, is all that is required. In practice, however, these conditions rarely exist. Budgetary control is an imperfect tool that can assist in controlling situations that are complex and uncertain. It will never be completely effective, but it may be important and useful to management.

Reference: Drury, C. (1988)

Further reading: Hopwood, A.G. (1974)

5. Let the probability distribution of factory output be Normal with mean μ and standard deviation σ. A budget (b) having a 25% chance of attainment can be shown (from tables of the Normal distribution) to lie k standard deviations above the mean, where k = 0.675.

i.e. $b = \mu + k\sigma$

The sum of N such budgets will be

$Nb = N\mu + Nk\sigma$

and such a sum will be distributed normally with a mean of $N\mu$ and a standard deviation of $\sqrt{N}.\sigma$

The aggregate budget (Nb) thus lies $\sqrt{N}.k$ standard deviations above its mean. As N = 10 and k = 0.675, $\sqrt{N}k = 2.13$, and has only a 1.66% chance of being attained.

Reference: Otley, D.T. and Berry A.J. (1979)

Further reading: Livingstone, J.L. (ed), (1975)

6. Information that is intended to serve an attention directing function must be produced on a regular, routine basis, and have appropriate standards of comparison reported with it. Budget reports are an obvious example, but a variety of other information such as trends sales (having an implicit comparison with past periods), projected financial plans (compared with some desired future state) or comparisons with competitors all have a role to play. The objective of such reports is <u>not</u> to suggest solutions (although they may contain helpful information for this purpose) but rather to draw attention to problems or potential problems.

By contrast, problem-solving information is usually <u>ad hoc</u> and collected with a specific purpose in mind. For example, the impact of meeting a competitor head-on by cutting prices might be evaluated. Such a prediction would require an assessment of the competitor's likely reactions to the price cut (e.g. a price war) as well as the more usual cost and revenue data. Although routinely collected data may be an important resource in constructing such estimates, it is never sufficient and special costing exercises are inevitably involved in problem-solving activity.

The role of accounting information in the evaluation of performance (both the economic performance of a business unit and the overall performance of the manager) is more subtle. Accounting information captures only one aspect of performance and focuses on quantitatively measurable factors. Further, accounting measures of performance tend to be oriented to the short-term rather than the longer-term. Managerial performance evaluation requires the areas of responsibility of individual managers to be defined, which is often difficult in situations where managers are highly inter-dependent.

Reference: Part III of this book deals with many of these issues.

Further reading: Horngren, C.T. (1982)

7. The main danger in this situation lies in jumping to the conclusion that the division that fails to meet its budget targets is less successful than divisions that succeed in meeting their budget targets. Once such an assumption is made, and the necessity of achieving budget targets is communicated to the division, it is unlikely that it, too, will achieve its targets, but in potentially undesirable ways (see question 7.8).

The question that must be asked is what level of performance do the budget standards in each division represent? Are they truly comparable across all divisions or, more likely, does the level of difficulty vary from division to division? For example, it may be that the division which fails to meet its targets, is using the budget as a motivational device, set at a challenging level of performance. It may not expect managers to achieve the targets set, but use them to generate the best possible level of actual performance. On the other hand, it may really be disorganized and inefficient.

Such a judgement can only be made on the basis of extensive comparisons, both internally within the organization concerned and externally with competing firms in the same line of business. For example, a full set of accounting ratios, comparing the division with other divisions (inevitably in other lines of business) and with other similar firms, would be invaluable. If the result was a judgement that the division concerned was efficient and well run, it might be that a tightening of budget targets in other divisions, and an evaluation of their performance would be an appropriate course of action.

Reference: Otley, D.T. (1977), Chapters 4-6

Further reading: Otley, D.T. (1978)

80

8. There are essentially three methods of attaining budget targets in a way that was not expected when the targets were set.

These are :

(a) Affecting the level of the budget target itself, using the degree of consultation or participation offered as a means of reducing the standard demanded.

(b) Manipulating the accounting information that is reported (e.g. by charging incorrect accounts, by diverting expenditure from one account to another, by incorrect recording of time sheets, etc).

(c) By changing actual behaviour, usually in undesirable ways (e.g. by reducing expenditure on maintenance, by reducing service to other departments, by stressing short-term performance despite long-term costs).

The first method is the most difficult to detect and avoid. The setting of an appropriate budget standard requires trust to exist between superior and subordinate; the reaction of the superior to budget variances is critical to the effectiveness of setting future targets. The second method can be largely controlled by effective accounting system design, although it is always possible at the point of initial data entry. The third method is one that must be constantly monitored by superior managers; accounting information cannot be the sole measure of performance. Other indicators are essential if such dysfunctional behaviour is to be avoided. Overall, the superior manager's style of budget use is critical in determining subordinates' reactions.

Reference: Otley, D.T. (1977), Chapters 4-6

Further Reading: Chenhall, R.H. et al (1981)

9. The three managers evidently have quite different views of the function of budget estimates. The Marketing Manager is primarily concerned to set his salesmen motivating targets so that they are continually attempting to achieve them. He has evidently used these sales quotas as his input into the budgetary system, despite realizing that he does not expect them to be met most of the time. The Production Manager has behaved similarly, but with the difference that he has used ideal standards as his budget estimates. That is, he has submitted estimates of what might be achieved if everything worked out according to plan, whilst knowing that it usually did not. However, he is much more inclined to judge the firm's actual performance against past history rather than in comparison with the budget, which he knows is not likely to be achieved. The Accountant finds the attitudes of these managers to his budget system quite unacceptable. He needs the budget estimates in order to conduct financial planning to ensure that future financial needs are met. For this he requires the best estimates of what is expected to happen, not hopes of what might be achieved some of the time. We thus have the classic conflict between the use of budgets as targets designed to motivate improved performance and budgets as expectations designed to act as a basis for planning. Evidently the same set of figures cannot serve both purposes adequately.

There are a wide variety of possible solutions to reconciling these conflicting purposes. Perhaps the Marketing Manager could keep his sales quotas, but use his estimate of likely out-turns as his input to the budget system. Similarly the Production Manager could set his own factory standards and targets, but use expected actuals (may be based on previous years' results) for budgeting. This would produce a budget that was useful for the Accountant's purposes of financial planning. However, the budget would be of little use for other purposes if this was done. If it was considered desirable to have budgets for junior managers, and it was thought that these should represent targets to be aimed at rather than expectations of actual outcome. Thus we may have a single budget that is a motivational target to junior operating managers yet is adjusted to be a planning tool for senior managers.

In reality budgets serve multiple purposes, some being served rather more adequately than others. The challenge to the budget system designer is to balance these potentially conflicting purposes in a way that meets the particular needs of his own organization.

10. (a) Quite clearly both divisional managers have acted against the best interests of the company. Division A has taken on projects yielding additional profits of £50 000 by investing an additional £600 000 (ignoring depreciation), an accounting rate of return of just over 8% and less than the company's cost of capital. Division B, on the other hand has reduced its profits by £25 000 by cutting out investment of £200 000. The average rate of return on this investment of 12% is in excess of the company's cost of capital and greatly in excess of the return on the new investments made by Division A.

The effect of both decisions can be seen most graphically if residual income (profit less a notional charge for capital employed at 10%) is computed:

	Division A	Division B
Last year	(£50 000)	£25 000
This year	(£60 000)	£20 000

In both cases the residual income has been reduced by the actions taken, indicating that they are undesirable despite the improved rate of return both generate.

(b) Part of the Chief Executive's problem was caused by the imprecision of his statement exhorting divisional managers to 'improve their divisional profitability'. It is not clear whether he wanted increased profit or increased return on investment. In fact both can be undesirable as the circumstances outlined in the question indicate. Higher profits at the cost of a low return on investment, or a higher return on investment but lower profits may both be against the interests of the company. If having a single measure of performance is considered to be important then residual income avoids these defects of accounting profit and return on capital employed. Alternatively, accounting profit could be used together with strict central controls on divisional investment and disinvestment decisions. Further, it may well be wise to develop budget targets which unambiguously define what is required rather than generalized exhortations to improve.

However, the development of budgets for a single measure of performance such as accounting profit or residual income is unlikely to be a complete answer. Distortions may be built into the process by managers attempting to bias budget estimates in their favour so as to make them easier to attain; strict accountability to an annual target may also encourage 'creative' accounting techniques, and also the neglect of certain desirable activities, such as repairs and maintenance expenditure, designed to show favourable accounting performance. Such undesirable side effects can be minimized by considering a wider range of performance measures, such as those developed by the General Electric Company. There the following items of performance were measured and evaluated:

1. Profitability
2. Market position
3. Productivity
4. Product leadership
5. Personnel development
6. Employee attitudes
7. Public responsibility

8. Balance between short-range and long-range goals.

The last item in this list indicates one issue that can rarely be stated once and for all.   There is always a trade-off between current performance and future performance, and divisional managers need to know which they ought to emphasize at any one time. Perhaps this is one area where the development of formal goals and measures is less important than the discussion of the general issues with the managers concerned.

Reference: Dearden, J. (1960)

Further reading: Henderson, B.D. and Dearden, J. (1966)

CHAPTER 8

PLANNING AND CONTROL IN A COMPLEX AND UNCERTAIN WORLD

1. The structural causes of non-programmed decisions are:

    (a) the adoption of the multidivisional organization structure.

    (b) the decentralization of decision-making within the multidivisional company.

    Both of these can be seen as logical responses to environmental uncertainty and the complexity/diversity of organizational activities.

    The attributes of non-programmed decisions can be measured along several dimensions.   The following list affords a comparison with the attributes of programmed decisions at the extreme.

Non-programmed decisions	Programmed decisions
Unique	Repetitive
Change over time	Stable over time
No quantifiable expectations of performance	Predictable performance
Novel	Well understood and specified
Informal, intuitive models	Formal models can be used for planning
Intuitive control	Control by measuring quantified deviations from expectation
Judgement is essential	Need for independent judgement is minimal

| No standards of performance are totally appropriate | Well-established performance criteria and measures of efficiency are available. |

With these attributes in mind, students should answer parts (a) through (f) making their assumptions clearly and matching them with the attributes above. The following suggestions are therefore heavily dependent on the assumptions made and seek to establish the view that decision takers face more or less programmed decisions, that is, that a continuum exists between the extremes.

(a) Programmed — Men, materials, advertising, lay-out and service determined by the franchiser not the local manager.

(b) Non-programmed — The uncertainty inherent in the task calls for novel decision taking. Applied research may exhibit attributes more consistent with programmed tasks.

(c) Programmed — Productivity is dependent on earlier stages of the production process and can be measured accurately and predictably.

(d) Non-programmed — This depends on the turbulence of the micro-computer market and the need for the manager to be capable to react to competitive pressures.

(e) Programmed — Taking the teaching perspective, the courses offered may not change over time, their content may be subject to only slight modification and the measurement of performance may follow well-established patterns.

(f) Non-programmed — Dependent upon the number of repetitive events organized by the club, past experience may be an inadequate guide of demand and hence the number of bar staff required.

Reference: Dermer, J. (1977)

Further reading: Hakanson, N. (1969) 'An Induced Theory of Accounting under

Risk', The Accounting Review, July, pp. 495-514.

2.   Information asymmetry relates to the uneven distribution of information within

the business enterprise. Top management (the principal) does not have the same

intimate knowledge of the operations of specific activities as divisional or lower level

management (the agent).

Principal-agent theory (PAT) explicitly recognizes that the agent is hired to

perform a task in an uncertain environment. Recognition of information asymmetry

may cause the principal to incur increased monitoring costs in an attempt to measure

the agent's effort more accurately. Alternatively or additionally, the agent may incur

bonding costs such as giving assurances to the principal that certain decisions will

not be taken or some aspects of the business will not change. Inevitably, because the

preferences or beliefs of the principal and agent cannot be consistently matched over

time, a residual loss occurs. The concern of PAT is to create an efficient, defined by

Pareto optimality, employment contract between the principal and agent.

There are two sets of problems associated with information asymmetry. Moral

hazard relates to the misrepresentation of outcomes in circumstances when it is costly

for the other party to judge outcomes. In the context of the multidivisional company,

top management will have to accept the accuracy of the information provided by the

divisions unless increased monitoring costs are incurred.   From a planning

perspective, the other set of problems termed adverse selection is most important.

Adverse selection relates to the misrepresentation of the true attributes or

qualities of a task under circumstances in which it is not possible for the other party

to determine the truth at low cost. A specific example is the budgeted sales level provided by a divisional manager. Top management cannot determine the degree of effort required of the divisional manager to meet this target; the accuracy and completeness of the divisional manager's predictive model is unknown. Unless the adverse selection problem can be overcome, feedback control is of limited usefulness. Hence, the recognition of adverse selection places the emphasis upon developing feasible feed-forward controls in order that top and divisional managers can agree certain actions as appropriate. Unfortunately, the AIS with its traditional emphasis on feedback controls may provide an incentive for divisional managers to bias their plans as targets.

Reference: Kaplan, R. (1982)

Further reading: Magee, R.P. (1980) 'Equilibria in Budget Participation',
Journal of Accounting Research, Autumn, pp. 551-573.

3. In the unitary structured firm, sub-goal pursuit may be caused by:
    (a) The difficulty of developing goals or targets for the functional parts which easily translate to the company's goals or targets.
    (b) Intentional bias because the functional manager believes he has prime responsibility for the welfare of his activity and only partial and ill-defined responsibility for overall company goals.
    (c) The accuracy of communication from the top management is subject to interpretation and filtering at successive levels of the hierarchy.

The adoption of the multidivisional organization structure allows the divisions to follow goals or targets expressed in terms consistent with the overall company's goals. Also, the number of hierarchical levels through which information is transmitted is reduced. However, the promotion of divisional interests at the expense of the company may increase.

89

The creation of separate divisions may increase different orientations, beliefs and preferences within divisional management. The multidivisional structure may promote parochial attitudes and an over-competitive atmosphere internally resulting in the divisions not interacting when opportunities arise. The presence of an AIS which measures separate divisional performance may strengthen the internal competitiveness. Co-operation may be sacrificed in order to disadvantage a sister division.

Information asymmetry and the relatively high incidence of non-programmed decisions allows divisional managers considerable opportunities to pursue sub-goals with little fear of detection. The linking of incentive schemes with the AIS performance measures provides the reason to introduce bias and to manipulate accounting reports.

Reference: Williamson, O.E. (1975)

Further reading: Groves T. and M. Loeb (1970) 'Incentives in Divisionalized Firms', Management Science, March, pp. 221-230.

4.   Through participation, the relevance of targets incorporated in the budget may be improved. The more relevant the target, the greater the likelihood that the manager will internalize it and become committed to its achievement. Unfortunately, participation in budget setting may result in relatively easy targets being agreed. Bias may be introduced for a number of motives (Lowe and Shaw, 1968).

The bias may be intentional – to gain rewards linked to a comparison between actual and budgeted results, for approval–seeking purposes in the light of recent poor performance, or to comply with company conventions such as a normal growth in sales of 2% per annum. In addition, the target may be subject to unintentional bias because of the inherent uncertainty associated with the environment or task undertaken. The detection of bias through participation is very difficult because it may be intentional or unintentional, optimistic or pessimistic.

In the multidivisional structure, where the incidence of non-programmed decisions is likely to be relatively high and where information asymmetry persists, the need for participation appears essential. The divisional managers are likely to possess the most accurate predictive models of the division's activities and their associated uncertain environments. Hence, divisional management's involvement in planning operations and budget setting seems essential if relevant targets are to emerge. However, it is precisely in these circumstances that bias and the creation of organizational slack may occur with little or no chance of detection. The AIS therefore needs to remove any incentives divisional managers may have to misuse true participation. Ensuring that performance is not gauged solely by comparing actual and budgeted financial results may remove this motive to bias. Extending the time scale over which performance is evaluated to reveal a trend of results may reduce the motivation to bias for approval seeking purposes. Increasing the dimensions by which performance is gauged to include non-financial quantitative and qualitative measures may help to reduce the emphasis placed on meeting company norms. By these means the motives to bias may be overcome and participation to determine relevant standards or targets may be attained.

Reference: Hofstede, G. (1968)

Further reading: Flamholtz, E.G. (1983) 'Accounting, Budgeting and Control Systems in their Organizational Context' Accounting, Organizations and Society, July, pp. 153-169.

5. Fundamentally, the traditional AIS assumes that the necessary conditions of the cybernetic control model exist in reality. That is:

(a) There is a clear objective.

(b) The output can be accurately measured in terms of the dimensions defined by the objective.

(c) A predictive model is required to explain non-attainment of the objective and to suggest corrective actions.

(d) Alternative actions are available to reduce deviations from the objective.

In the context of planning, conditions 1 and 3 are perhaps the most important. Agreement on the objective of a business enterprise is as much an exercise in political bargaining as economic reasoning. In social systems, the objectives may be transient, ill specified and non-quantifiable. When the enterprise faces a high incidence of non-programmed decisions, agreement on objectives must involve lower level managers if infeasible objectives are to be avoided. Achieving consensus about objectives may become more difficult because of widening the participating groups whose interests and preferences may converge only by coincidence.

The involvement of lower level managers is necessitated and substantiated by their possession of the most accurate predictive models relating to parts of the business operations. The characteristics of non-programmed decisions implies the need for judgement and intuition. Top management cannot possess this information except by incurring substantial costs and current budgeting procedures are not sufficient to uncover the specific predictive model being used.

In order to improve planning in these situations, there must be an incentive for lower level managers to provide honest, unbiased targets. Or, at the very least, the AIS must not provide incentives to bias targets. Withdrawing any strict reward link with actual and budgeted comparisons and de-emphasizing short-term evaluation may reduce the motivation to bias. More positively, the planning of non-programmed decisions should be undertaken with a richer data base in a democratic atmosphere. Top management should supply the assumptions on which corporate strategies are based and lower level management should substantiate their financial plans by reference to operating and environmental assumptions. Feed-forward controls should concentrate on differences in the sets of assumptions and the accountant's role should be extended to monitor key assumptions and to report changes to both management levels. The importance of external variables and events should focus lower and top managements' attention on the environment. If the iterative questioning of the planning assumptions is carried out in a supportive, democratic fashion, the use of accounting data to control or to attach blame for non-attainment may be replaced by its use for self-control. Feasible actions may be planned which explicitly acknowledge the uncertainty of a changing environment. The accounting information contained in the budget is not seen as an end in itself but merely a translation of expected events given an agreed set of assumptions. It may be argued that a comparison of the expected assumptions and what actually transpired is of equal importance to any comparison conducted in financial terms.

Reference: Dyckman, T.R. (1975)

Further reading: Ijiri, Y., J. Kinard and F. Putney (1968) 'An Integrated Evaluation System for Budget Forecasting and Operating Performance with a Classified Budgeting Bibliography', Journal of Accounting Research, Spring, pp. 1-28.

6. (a) Participation in budget setting.

Arguments for participation can include greater commitment to the budget target, more relevant targets, improved communication and, in providing a specified target, may improve performance. However, the empirical evidence (Brownell, 1981; Hirst 1981, etc) suggests that universal benefits of participation are unlikely.

Participation may be used to bias budgets for a number of reasons. Approval seeing behaviour, conforming with corporate conventions or norms about growth and ensuring rewards are some of the potential reactions (Lowe and Shaw, 1968). The direction and magnitude of the manipulation may be difficult to detect in order to apply counter-bias.

Recognition of the degree of uncertainty or the subsequent level of non-programmed decision-making the manager undertakes, suggests that participation is essential when uncertainty (non-programmability) is high. The reverse may be true when uncertainty is low.

(b) A 16% chance of attainment indicates that the estimates are one standard deviation from their mean. When added together, the aggregate is distributed with a mean of 8100 and a standard deviation of 427 ($E\sqrt{\theta i}^2 = 427$).

Total $= \dfrac{9360 - 8100}{427} = 2.95$ standard deviations from mean

a probability of 0.2% that total output will be attained.

The corporate management adjustment allowing a 16% chance of attainment (or one standard deviation) means that total expected output becomes $8100 + 427 = 8527$. The pro rata adjustment and the probabilities of unit managers attaining these adjusted targets are given below.

Unit	Expected Output	Standard Deviation	Submitted Estimate	Reduced Estimate	z value	Probability
A	500	100	600	547	0.47	32 %
B	600	110	710	647	0.43	33
C	700	120	820	747	0.39	35
D	800	130	930	847	0.36	36
E	900	140	1040	947	0.34	37
F	1000	150	1150	1048	0.32	37.5
G	1100	160	1260	1148	0.3	38
H	1200	170	1370	1248	0.28	39
I	1300	180	1480	1348	0.27	39
	8100	427	9360	8527		

If budgets are non-mean estimates — either optimistic or pessimistic — then care is needed when aggregating because an extreme total budget may result. Pro rata adjustment can be inequitable. Either more sophisticated methods should be used or budgets should not be required to add up.

(c) Control loss may arise from problems encountered in communication, co-ordination and opportunistic behaviour. Communication difficulties arise because the number of channels expand disproportionately $[1/2(M^2 - M)]$ and due to filtering over successive hierarchical levels. Growth by means of adding more specialized functional posts to the unitary or functional organization structure is thereby inhibited in its effectiveness.

Co-ordination problems stem from the aggregation issue but also from the translation of corporate goals into operational financial targets for separate parts of the functionally organized company. The corporate goal of say, profit may need to be expressed into a cost target of £x per unit of output for a process or production unit and into £y revenue for a marketing unit. Growth in the number of separate functions and separate performance measures may cause difficulties in synchronizing activity levels. The extent to which managers perceive the separate performance measures as ends in themselves as opposed to means to an end may be a deciding factor.

Opportunistic behaviour recognizes the parochial or self-interest attitude managers may adopt. By meeting targets or financial performance measures in the short term, some managers may reap rewards at the expense of other functions.

The multidivisional structure is likely to mitigate but not entirely eliminate the worst excesses associated with the communication and co-ordination problems. However, the multidivisional structure highlights the need for separate performance measures and may exacerbate the opportunistic behaviour problem. To attain their performance, individual divisional managers may indulge in harmful practices (reallocation, transfer pricing, etc) for the company which apparently show the division in a favourable light.

7. Eaglet plc

A balanced dealership suggests that each activity is free to compete in its own product-market. A diversified strategy is being followed and the distinctiveness of the three markets is being highlighted. Hence, the immediate concern of the AIS is to provide information about the separate activities. The first, and perhaps the most fundamental problem, to be encountered is how to develop separate, relevant plans and targets for the activities.

96

The manager of the new cars operation may justifiably argue that his projected sales heavily depends on the trade-in values the used car manager is willing to offer to prospective new car purchasers. The used car manager may argue that his projected profit is heavily dependent on the charges for repairs made by the service manager. The force of these arguments may be reduced if all three managers are free to use external suppliers and such services are readily available. The environment must be monitored not only in this respect but also to discover whether in fact new cars, used cars and repair servicing constitute separate markets.

When the emphasis is placed on the new car sales operation, this implies that the other two activities are co-ordinated to ensure increased new car sales. The used car manager will consult with the new car manager to determine an acceptable buying-in price. Likewise, the service manager will give priority to new car after sales maintenance to ensure customer satisfaction. The AIS needs only to record total profitability for the enterprise because the individual activities' performance is heavily influenced by integrative policies. There remains the need to scan the environment with particular regard to factors which are thought to influence new car sales.

The emphasis on the used car operation similarly requires increased co-ordination between this and the repairs activity. However, because the used car activity usually precedes new car sales, the manager of used cars will have no incentive to offer attractive buying-in prices if the concern is to re-sell used cars. Hence, new cars may find that this strategy increases the price differential between new and used cars and adversely affects the viability of this operation. The AIS may need to prepare separate financial reports and plans for new cars and the combination of the used cars and repair servicing. Two environments therefore need to be monitored, used cars and new cars. The plans for each can be undertaken separately.

Under each alternative strategy, individual managers experience different degrees of discretion to make decisions. When other than the balanced dealership is pursued, the need to co-ordinate reduces some managers' discretion. In so doing, the non-programmed decision becomes more stable and hence more programmed. When a balanced dealership is emphasized, all three managers face non-programmed decisions which may be appropriate if the three activities do indeed serve distinct market environments.

Reference: Lawrence P.R. and Lorsch J.W. (1967a)

Implications for AIS

Whilst planning is affected by the combination of strategy and structure adopted, the appropriateness of certain financial performance measures is also conditioned by the combination.

Under the balanced dealership, the need for separate performance measures for each activity is paramount. A comparison of budgeted and actual profit seems appropriate and if each manager has discretion over the working capital decision, ROI and RI may be used. The garage repairs manager may control the stock of spare parts, exhausts, tyres, etc; the used and new cars managers may control the number of cars they respectively have on show.

With the new car emphasis and the need to co-ordinate garage services and used car sales to improve new car sales and profitability, different financial performance measures are needed. Garage services may best be regarded as a cost centre, the manager being evaluated by means of a comparison of the budgeted and actual costs he controls. Used cars may be viewed as a revenue centre because the cost of cars traded-in will not be subject to this manager's discretion. Alternatively, the repair work performed on used cars and authorized by the used cars manager may suggest a limited profit responsibility. New cars may be regarded as a profit centre but even this depends on the discretionary decision-making this manager has over repair costs and trade-in costs.

With the used car emphasis, garage repairs may remain a cost centre, new cars a revenue centre and used cars a profit centre. Under all three strategies but especially the last two, non-financial quantitative performance measures appear useful. For garage repairs, measures of idle time or throughput may be developed; for used cars, the number of warranties activated or complaints are useful additions. For new cars, the number of repeat customers should be monitored.

In this relatively simple example, many of the complexities of matching the appropriate AIS to the organizational circumstances can be explored.

References: Vancil R.F. 'What Kind of Management Control Do You Need?' Harvard Business Review, Mar/April 1973.

8. Sennapods

(a)

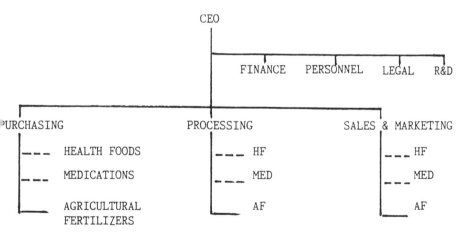

Presumably purchasing will contain a quality inspection unit. Some purchases may be common to all three product ranges but vary only in quality or refinement. Sales and marketing for the three product ranges should be differentiated to recognize the different types of customer e.g. NHS, farmers and co-operatives, health food retailers.

Control loss in terms of communication, co-ordination and opportunistic behaviour may be encountered as additional levels are added to the management hierarchy. For example, a change in NHS requirements needs to be communicated to the CEO from sales and marketing and back down to purchasing and processing. Filtering of information and the number of communication channels will increase as the levels in the management hierarchy expand.

Co-ordination will become more difficult as managers with differing degrees of optimism and pessimism find their targets aggregated. Translation of corporate financial targets to operational revenue and/or cost targets can also cause difficulties.

Opportunistic behaviour and parochial interest may be increased as processing managers become more concerned with the professional engineering qualities of the equipment as opposed to providing an output at a price which ensures increased sales perhaps.

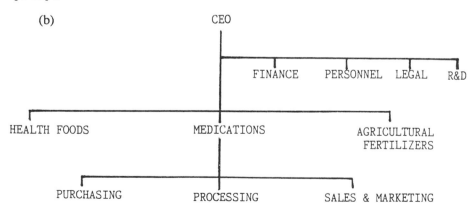

(b)

This structure reduces the levels of management before the decision-maker is reached; each division can be given the same objective as the company but simply because each division's individual performance is highlighted, the incentive for opportunistic behaviour may be increased.

Advantages also include the training of general, rather than functional, managers, greater commitment to a product-market environment, improved co-ordination and a distinction of roles, allowing top management to concentrate on strategic planning.

Against these there are increased costs due to duplication of resources, high quality top management and staff required, an incentive scheme for divisional managers, and the possibility that decentralization may mean managers will not take decisions in the company's best interests. Cross-fertilization of ideas and techniques may prove more difficult under the multidivisional structure.

(c) Several approaches are available but a common element is that under the multidivisional structure the main divisions can be made responsible for profit. Hence, profit (or investment) centres may be the norm under the multidivisional structure whereas under a functional organization, cost or revenue responsibility may be the norm. Both systems should employ a budgeted comparison with actuals.

Problems of interdependence may be more easily catered for under a cost centre system whereas under the profit centre system, transfer pricing can cause severe problems. Allocations may affect both situations. All of these impact on the feedback controls resulting from comparisons of budgeted and actual performance.

Of equal importance is the extent of feed-forward controls. Under the multidivisional structure, it seems essential that divisional managers participate fully in setting targets because they are more knowledgeable of the environment. The same degree of participation may actually be counter-productive in the functional setting.

Linking incentives or rewards to comparisons of financial performance may provide positive motivation when the manager has not participated in setting targets. This rigid link in the multidivisional structure could encourage managers to create budget slack.

Consistent with the foregoing, a short-term evaluation along the lines of the budget constrained style may be effective in the functional organization. For the multidivisional structure, a longer-term trend analysis utilizing measures additional to financial performance measures appears appropriate.

CHAPTER 9

PERFORMANCE MEASUREMENT AND EVALUATION

1. All financial performance measures can be argued to suffer from limitations of completeness, accuracy and neutrality. They are incomplete because by definition they measure only those aspects of managerial or economic performance which are quantifiable in financial terms. In addition, the measurement usually relates to only the short-term and, in aggregate form, it may conceal information about how parts of the enterprise interact. The accuracy of financial performance measures is spurious in that the application of generally accepted accounting principles can result in different income figures. Even so, deviations between expected and actual financial performance measures are capable of ambiguous interpretation because the measures reflect a mix of outcomes, some of which are caused by the environment and by other managerial decisions within the firm. The accuracy of the targeted performance measure depends on the stability of the decision environment and how well established the predictive model is. When these conditions don't apply, the performance measure may be subject to political, self-interested manipulation. Due to the use of financial performance measures to control or reward managers, it must be recognized that managers are not indifferent to the score that is recorded for themselves or their divisions. Opportunisitic behaviour to benefit at another division's expense and to make decisions which apparently improve the performance measure now at the expense of longer-term gains may be expected.

The choice between RI and ROI is little affected by calculating profit pre- or post-tax, pre- or post-depreciation, measuring asset values pre- or post-depreciation and basing asset values or historic or current costs. By and large, RI may be argued to be conceptually superior to ROI but ROI has technical advantages over RI.

The conceptual advantages of RI over ROI are :

(a) more precise guidelines for planning

(b) measures for the unit (net RI) and the manager (controllable RI)

(c) flexibility in that the cost of capital may be changed for different divisions or different types of assets

(d) promotes cost awareness of the use of assets by divisional managers

(e) provides greater consistency between how short-term and long-term decisions are taken e.g. RI implies a decision rule to maximize return above a given cost of capital as opposed to maximize the rate of return on investment.

The technical advantages of ROI over RI are :

(a) normally controllable and non-controllable investment bases are not required to be distinguished

(b) the calculation of cost of capital is avoided

(c) easily understood and in common use

(d) comparable between divisions of the same company if there are uniform accounting policies.

There is broad agreement that controllable profit or controllable contribution is an appropriate performance measure for profit centre managers. When the manager does not control the investment base, ROI gives exactly the same signal as controllable profit. RI on the other hand would not (Amey, 1969). However, the situation where the disadvantages and advantages outlined above would have greater importance is when the manager controls or significantly influences the investment base. For true investment centre managers, the relatively unambiguous guideline which RI provides plus its potential consistency with DCF investment appraisal techniques may make it preferable.

Reference :   Emmanuel, C.R. and D.T. Otley (1976)

Further reading :   Tomkins, C. (1980) 'Financial Planning and Control in Large Companies', in Arnold, Carsberg and Scapens (eds.) <u>Topics in Management Accounting</u>, Philip Allan, pp. 241-261.

2.   In the context of student evaluation, there are basically two reactions. Firstly, the student may enquire of the lecturer how the coursework is assessed and may try to convince the lecturer of the merits of the alternative approach taken. If this fails, the student may adopt the lecturer's approach or values in order to obtain better grades. Alternatively, the student may be convinced of the approach he has taken and will lower his aspiration levels, that is expect to be awarded lower grades. Secondly, the student may react more radically by non-attendance of lectures or tutorials or by non-submission of coursework in the belief that whatever he does, the grade will not reflect the effort he has expended.

Similar reactions are likely in the case of the divisional manager. Attempts to convince top management that the evaluation procedure is unfair in his situation may go unheeded if support from other managers is not forthcoming. Ignoring the evaluation procedure entirely is a high risk alternative for the manager because the company appears to give some significance to financial results. The least troublesome action for the manager is to manipulate actual performance, or reports of actual performance so that they accord with the financial targets.

In both situations, there is the danger of participants 'playing the system' or the system isolating the individual to the point of non-involvement. Modifications are difficult to recommend but it may be appropriate that top management seeks to understand the problems of the manager. If the manager is experiencing peculiar difficulties, then additional measures of performance along these dimensions may be inaugurated. Top management should also take the opportunity to explain the full workings of the evaluation procedure. Personal fears, prejudices perceived by the manager may be allayed if the details of how people are rewarded/promoted, etc., are disclosed openly in some detail.

Reference : Brownell, P. (1981)

3. This example illustrates the allocation problem. The crucial element is the estimate of the professor's time which is to be spent on the research project. On this basis the three main cost elements in the research grant are determined.

From the professor's perspective, the estimate of time to be spent on the research project is the only input in the grant request which he controls. If he wants the project funded under this system, the estimate of time will be pared to the minimum feasible level. However, even the most well thought out research project encounters unforeseen problems and an additional request for funds may not prove successful.

From the administration's perspective, the system may appear quite reasonable. Research requests include an element to contribute to the facilities which the university has provided, both at the centre and at the department. However, the central administration would prefer to have a bigger number of hours to be spent on the research project than a smaller number thereby recouping in absolute terms a larger contribution to overheads. From the administration's viewpoint, the concern is not that every project is funded but that the average success rate is sufficient to cover overheads.

The research agency under this procedure may pronounce whether the central and overhead charges are reasonable. Are these charges fair? This very much depends on the initial estimate of hours to be spent on the project supplied by the professor. This is the crucial question.

Presumably professor X could estimate the time spent on teaching, attending committee meetings and performing research. Unfortunately, the activity compartments are not water-tight. Some of the time spent on research will involve training a research assistant. As principal investigator, some portion of time is spent administrating the research grant. The research will no doubt give rise to lecture material and new teaching courses. Although the professor's time spent on research appears traceable to this activity, it is by no means clear how much of this time is specifically devoted to research.

The same argument applies to head office functions like top management salaries, the cost of the central finance office or personnel department. Will the subsequent allocations of these costs to divisions or production departments be equitable if the time spent on one activity's problems apply to other activities?

Any comparison of actual with budgeted costs is worthless. The allocation basis is incorrigible – unverifiable and irrefutable – and the financial results are merely a reflection of this.

Reference : Thomas, A.L. (1980b)

Further reading : Thomas, A.L. (1982) 'Reporting of Faculty Time: An Accounting Perspective', <u>Science</u>, January, pp. 27-32.

4. (a) Book profit of each product.

i) **NRV**

	Toaster	Washing Machine	Electric Carvers	Tumble Driers	TOTAL
Net realizable value	(5)K	1K	79K	154K	229K
Allocated costs	(2.2)	.4	34.5	67.3	100
Book Profit	(2.8)	.6	44.5	86.7	129

ii) **Democratic**

	Toaster	Washing Machine	Electric Carvers	Tumble Driers	TOTAL
Contribution	(5)K	1K	79K	154K	229K
Allocated costs	25	25	25	25	100
Book Profit	(30)	(24)	54	129	129

(b) Book profit of each product with improved efficiency.

i) **NRV**

Net realizable value	3K	1K	79K	154K	237K
Allocated	1.3	.4	33.3	65	100
Book Profit	1.7	.6	45.7	89	137

ii) **Democratic**

Contribution	3K	1K	79K	154K	237K
Allocated costs	25	25	25	25	100
Book Profit	(22)	(24)	54	129	137

(c) Book profit of each product with increased selling price.

The book profits are exactly the same as in (b i) and (b ii) above.

(d) In the first case, the NRV method ensures that each product's book profits are proportional to each product's contribution. It is apparent that toasters should be discontinued but under the Democratic allocation method, washing machines also appear as possible candidates for discontinuation. It may be argued that any incentive scheme should be linked with book profits determined under the NRV method.

However, in the second case when toasters have improved the efficiency of production, the NRV method results in two other product divisions also showing improved book profits. If the timing of these cases were reversed, electric carvers and tumble driers would show reduced profits purely because of actions undertaken by another division over which they have no control. The same effect on book profit is again recorded when toasters increase the selling price. Under NRV, the other division's book profits increase due to a decision taken in another division. Only the Democratic method results in stable book profits being recorded regardless of the changes. It is behaviour congruent in the sense that efficiencies or deficiencies in other parts of the company do not affect the profit reported. Hence, any incentive scheme linked to book profits must be aware of the dangers of allocating joint costs. No one method is satisfactory as this example illustrates.

Reference : Thomas, A.L. (1980b)

Further reading Zimmerman, J.L. (1979) 'The Costs and Benefits of Cost Allocations' <u>The Accounting Review</u>, July, pp. 504-521.

5. (a)		Grand Slam		Triple Crown	
Total Investment	Cost of Capital	ROI	RI	ROI	RI
£3000K	£900K	33%	£100K	6%	(720)K
4000	1200	50	800	12	(720)
5000	1500	60	1500	15	(750)
6000	1800	62.5	1950	18	(720)
7000	2100	64.3	2400	25	(350)
8000	2400	62.5	2600	20	(800)
9000	2700	61.1	2800	15	(1350)
10000	3000	58	2800	12	(1800)
11000	3300	54.5	2700	10	(2200)
12000	3600	51.7	2600	8	(2640)

Both managers set targets in ROI terms which they knew they could beat if the investment base is under their control and can be changed in the short term. In both cases the investment base can be varied between £5–£9 million and the targeted ROI can be attained or bettered.

(b) The RI target consistent with the 60% ROI expected of the Grand Slam division is given unambiguously as £1.5 million. If the actual ROI attained of 64.3% is consistent with the £7 million investment level, a favourable RI variance of £900 000 would be recorded abstracting from depreciation charges. For the Triple Crown division, the targeted ROI translates to either a negative RI of £755 000 or £1 350 000. If the intention was to guide the manager to the £5 million investment level, a zero variance on RI would indicate that this has been achieved. However, if he has

110

remained at the £9 million level, an adverse variance of £600 000 would be shown. ROI on the other hand, would merely show that the 15% is achieved and that no action needs to be taken.

(c) Total Investment	Cost of Capital		Grand Slam	Triple Crown
	at 60%	at 15%	RI	RI
£3000K	£1800K	£ 450K	£ (800)K	£ (270)K
4000	2400	600	(400)	(120)
5000	3000	750	0	0
6000	3600	900	150	80
7000	4200	1050	300	700
8000	4800	1200	200	400
9000	5400	1350	100	0
10 000	6000	1500	(200)	(300)
11 000	6600	1650	(600)	(550)
12 000	7200	1800	(1000)	(840)

To maximize the absolute return in excess of the divisional cost of capital, both managers are directed to aim for an investment level of £7 million. Varying the investment base will not improve either manager's results and because RI is an absolute profit measure, any deviation will be reflected in the RI figures actually recorded.

Reference : Solomons, D. (1965)

6. (a) Blackstone Engineering Co. Ltd.

DIVISIONS

	A		B		C	
	£000		£000		£000	
Sales	9 000		6 450		5 250	
Less Direct prod. costs	4 500		3 000		2 400	
Direct exp.	1 350		750		600	
Selling exp.	900	6 750	600	4 350	300	3 300
Variable Profit		2 250		2 100		1 950
Less Controllable divisional overheads :						
Depreciation on controllable investment		510		385.5		247.5
R & D requested		112.5		225		112.5
Admin expenses		270		246		120
Financial expenses		150		150		180
		1 042.5		1 006.5		660
Controllable operating profit		1 207.5		1 093.5		1 290
Less interent on Controllable I		570		315		240
Controllable Residual Income before taxes		637.5		778.5		1 050

	A	B	C
	£000	£000	£000
Less non-controllable divisional overheads :			
Depreciation allocated	90	64.5	52.5
R & D	187.5	75	37.5
Admin expenses	180	129	105
Financial expenses	300	150	120
	757.5	418.5	315
Interest on non-controllable I	180	60	60
	937.5	478.5	375
Net Residual Income before taxes	(300)	300	675
Less C.T.	300	300	375
Net Residual Income after taxes	(600)	-	300
ROI : net profit after taxes capital employed	2%	10%	20%
Corporate ROI	8%		

(a) The same pattern of divisional performance is revealed by both the ROI and RI measures.

Whilst the ROI information may encourage complacency especially with regard to the operations of Division B (it meets the corporate cost of capital), the RI figures may prompt an investigation into a division which in absolute terms scores zero.

Illuminating data are contained in the controllable residual income information. These reveal that the divisional managers are controlling their operations relatively successfully. Inter-divisional comparisons on the basis of RI are to be avoided however because the measure tends to favour high investment divisions.

The main reasons for the individual divisions' ultimate performance lies with the method and impact of allocating HQ costs. On the net residual income basis, C's results are only 1.6 times better than A. The disparity is largely due to the company's allocation procedure.

Greater emphasis should be placed on an examination of centrally generated costs if the actual controllable incomes of the divisions meet their respective targets. These are perhaps the biggest omissions for evaluation purposes. Without budgets, inter-divisional comparisons especially on the basis of RI, are highly questionable.

(b) Practical arguments for the allocation of costs include discovering the 'true' profit of divisions or full cost of products or making divisional managers aware of common costs (BIM, 1974). Theoretical justifications for common cost allocations are offered by Zimmerman (1979). One justification states that over-consumption of perquisites is constrained by imposing effectively a lump sum tax on divisional managers. A second argument likens the allocations to opportunity cost proxies of 'difficult-to-observe' costs. The allocations constrain excessive misuse and therefore the quality of service is not degraded.

The conventional view is that all common cost allocations are incorrigible, that is, unverifiable and irrefutable. Decisions based on fully absorbed product costs or profits after allocations can be erroneous (Thomas, 1980b).

(c) By and large the theoretical advantages of RI over ROI are :

(i)   a separate measure of managerial and divisional performance consistent with responsibility accounting

(ii)   an income measure more consistent with economic income in that managers are made aware of the need to make a return on capital invested in the division

(iii)   a consistency with long-term evaluation models such as net present value when annuity depreciation and other conditions apply (see Chapter 12).

Practical advantages include :

(i)   a more precise target for planning and guiding the investment centre manager

(ii)   versatility in that different interest rates may be charged for working capital or different types of assets.

However, the practical difficulties of discovering controllable investment, appropriate costs of capital and overcoming user resistance to substituting a well known measure like ROI cannot be ignored.

7.   Cubic plc

(a) Discovering the individual cost of capital for each division should ensure that a balanced portfolio of capital projects are accepted by Cubic. The application of a universal cost of capital may result in high risk, high return divisions being favoured whilst low risk, low return divisions are discriminated against.

In addition, the use of the individual division's cost of capital for imputation of interest under RI or as a bench-mark of ROI introduces an external dimension by which to evaluate a division's performance.

(b)

i)   Divisional cost of capital

	Consumer Durable	Industrial Plant Hire	Leisure
Asset beta	0.8(0.9)=0.72	0.6(1.3)=0.78	0.7(1.9)=1.33
Required return	7+0.72(15-7)=12.76%	7+0.78(15-7)=13.24%	7+1.33(15-7)=17.64%
Cubic cost of Equity			
capital	0.6(0.72) +	0.2(0.78) +	0.2(1.33)=0.854
Required return	7+0.854(15-7)=13.832%		

ii)

	Consumer Durable	Industrial Plant Hire	Leisure
Asset beta	0.8(0.9)+0.2(0.3)=0.78	0.6(1.3)+0.4(0.3)=0.78	0.7(1.9)+0.3(0.3)=1.42
Required return	7+0.78(15-7)=13.24%	7+0.9(15-7)=14.2%	7+1.42(15-7)=18.36%
Cubic cost of Equity			
capital	0.6(0.78) +	0.2(0.9) +	0.2(1.42)=0.932
Require return	7+0.932(15-7)=14.456%		

The calculations rely on the assumption of the CAPM model which is essentially a single period model. Also R_m, the market portfolio, may be difficult to identify precisely and opinions may vary of R_f, the risk free rate of interest.

Identification of competitor companies operating in essentially the same markets at the same scale as the divisions may also prove problematic. Finally the question of exactly whose risk is incorporated in the required return or cost of capital needs to be addressed. Will the divisional manager's risk profile match that given by the CAPM when the individual competitor companies may be owner managed?

(c) When incorporated in short-term performance measures, the divisional costs of capital provide an external bench-mark for appraisal. However, these are only as appropriate as the match between the competitor company and the individual division. If, for some reason, the independent company is untypical in respect of the beta rating or its capital structure is unusual, the divisions may be faced with an inappropriate performance measure.

In favour of incorporating the divisional costs of capital into short-term performance measures are the features that more realistic targets may be set and the different markets, risk, profit and growth profiles of the individual divisions are to some extent recognized.

8. Cathcart Industries plc

(a) (i) The advantages of the unitary organization structure include :

1. ensuring a level of quality world-wide
2. emphasizing professional engineering and technology
3. perhaps maintaining a world-wide brand image or pricing policy.

Disadvantages may include :

1. top management have little time for strategy formulation
2. co-ordination of activities may be time-consuming and reacting to market changes slow

3.   emphasis on functions may lead to empire building and managers developing their sections with scant regard to corporate needs.

   (ii)   Advantages of multidivisional structure :

1.   closer attention paid to individual product markets and reaction to changes quicker

2.   top management free to plan strategy

3.   evaluation of separate parts of the business is possible.

   Disadvantages :

1.   opportunistic behaviour may be stimulated by separate performance measures

2.   the financial performance measures may be incomplete, inaccurate and non-neutral to some extent

3.   duplication of resources and increased costs due perhaps to incentive schemes etc.

(b)   A uniform cost of capital may result in the company investing in high return, high risk projects. Divisions which traditionally cannot meet these levels of return may be discriminated against. The use of specific costs of capital for each division should overcome this problem and may introduce a relevant external yardstick by which divisional performance should be evaluated.

(c)   Divisional cost of capital

Marine Engines

Asset beta	$0.7(1.5) = 1.05$
Required return	$9 + 1.05(18-9) = 18.45\%$ Equity
Asset beta	$0.7(1.5) + 0.3(0.3) = 1.14$
Required return	$9 + 1.14(18-9) = 19.26\%$ Debt and Equity

The assumptions relate to the CAPM model and to identifying the competitor company. Is the scale of operations, the market served etc. identical to the marine engine division?

CHAPTER 10

REWARDING MANAGERIAL PERFORMANCE

1. An approbation to 'Do what's best for the company' is definitely a motivational contract, but its terms are not very specific. Where nonspecific contracts are used, employees' evaluators have considerable discretion to decide whether the terms of the contract were followed. The contract has a motivational effect because subordinates attempt to infer what the vague statement means and how their evaluators will interpret it, and they act accordingly. Enforcement is provided through the standard organizational administrative mechanisms that are used to assign individuals' rewards (e.g. bonuses) and penalties.

2. The choices of the forms of compensation (both fixed and performance dependent) to offer managers involve trade-offs. Administration of the compensation contracts is easier and less costly if everyone is treated the same. But the value of the rewards to the individual managers is higher (for a given cost to the organization) if the managers are given the rewards which most closely suit their tastes. Designers must keep this basic conflict in mind as they are making their choices, but rarely does a simple answer to it exist.

3. Stock awards have a motivational effect if and only if the people to whom they are given attach a value to them. If the stock awards are seen as worthless, then promising them to managers will provide no motivational effect. Obviously stock

awards in firms with declining stock values are worth less than those in firms with appreciating stock values, and firms that are in decline will probably have to provide motivation through other forms of rewards (e.g. cash).

4. The present value calculation of a stream of annual rewards is clearly more valuable than a single accumulated reward received at the end of a five-year period. How large the deferred (end of five-year) payment would have to be to equalize the value of the annual payments depends on the discount rate one uses in making the present value calculation.

In deciding on a discount rate, the time value of money certainly has to be considered, but risk is potentially a greater concern. Risk is important because planning uncertainty usually increases sharply with the planning horizon. Thus even if managers say the one-year and five-year plans are equally difficult to achieve, they are usually referring to the midpoint of the distribution. The probability distribution surrounding the midpoint of the five-year plan will be broader, reflecting greater risk. The answers students give to the size of the promised long-term bonus opportunity that would equalize the value of the stream of annual incentive payments depends on their degree of risk aversion. Managers tend to think a deferred payment several times the sum of the annual payments is necessary to equalize the values.

5. Firms set lower performance cut-offs in their incentive compensation contracts because they do not want to pay bonuses for the generation of results they consider mediocre (or worse). The primary dangers in using these cut-offs are (1) that managers may 'take a bath', by loading all their expenses into a single period, when they are below the performance level necessary to earn a bonus payment, and (2) that

the total compensation of managers who are earning no incentive compensation through no fault of their own may fall below competitive levels and the result may be turnover.

6. Firms set upper cut-offs in their incentive compensation contracts for any of the reasons listed on p. 270 of the text. These cut-offs are typically most valuable in firms that have recently implemented or recently changed their incentive contracts. The cut-offs protect the firm from having to pay large bonuses for reasons related more to the misdesign of the contracts than to the effectiveness of the managers' actions.

But there are several dangers. The upper cut-offs may induce gameplaying, as managers may try to 'save' some of their performance (e.g. profits) until the subsequent period when they will be rewarded for it. The cut-offs may generate manager frustration with the unfairness of the evaluation process. And they may lead to turnover if managers (particularly the best ones) can find a firm that offers greater reward potentials.

7. Bonuses 'by formula' have the advantage of being quite explicit. Managers know exactly what is expected of them and how their rewards were assigned. And they do not have to worry about politics or other sources of bias in the evaluation process.

But it is not always possible to specify a formula that will reflect a manager's contribution for the period. Changing situations may render pre-specified performance standards and the weighting of various aspect of performance (e.g. current period profitability, growth) obsolete. Thus formulas may actually serve to reward managers for doing things that are no longer desirable.

8. A risk neutral manager would be indifferent to the two choices because the expected values are identical. A risk-averse manager would prefer (a), and a risk-loving manager would prefer (b). Since most people are risk-averse, firms that wish to provide performance-dependent rewards will have to promise higher expected compensation than those offering just straight salaries to keep their total compensation packages competitive.

CHAPTER 11

INTERDEPENDENCE AND TRANSFER PRICING

1.   The accountant's treatment of interdependence is to allocate costs or develop transfer prices. These responses have several common features. It is argued that the former allocates costs whilst the latter allocates profits to the segments of the business enterprise. The use of formulae to allocate costs, such as on the basis of the number of employees, sales revenue per division etc., have their equivalents in transfer price determination such as when a full cost plus a percentage or fixed amount of profit is used. Cost allocations and transfer prices may be decided by negotiation or by actual usage. In every case save one, the accounting responses carry implications for the discretionary authority of the segment manager. The manager must be unable to use an alternative source of supply or service and if this does not apply, the manager must supply unbiased and detailed information in order that an 'optimal' allocation or transfer price can be found. Hence, in a large number of cases, both transfer prices and cost allocations can be regarded as incorrigible — unverifiable and irrefutable – and unlikely to lead to behaviour congruence. Managers will have an incentive to manipulate the information they supply, to negotiate in an unco-operative manner or to mis-record the actual usage in order to improve their apparent financial performance.

The one case where transfer price determination and cost allocation can be distinguished occurs when the market test can be applied. An external market exists for the good or service which the segment uses. Corporate policy allows the manager to use this market and there are no quality or volume constraints inhibiting this use. However, intermediate markets are characterized by price and non-price competition and generally do not comply with the conditions of perfect competition. The use of market prices drawn from an imperfectly competitive market may result in managers taking sub-optimal decisions. Unfortunately attempts by the company to gauge the degree of imperfection will result in recentralization via the need for managers to supply detailed information on cost and revenue schedules. At this point it is worthwhile re-appraising why the business segments have quasi-autonomy. If the multidivisional structure is adopted to promote the diversification strategy, then flexible reaction to changing market conditions seems to be a significant necessity. By seeking optimal solutions, the company appears to be trying to isolate segments from market forces. Accountants and the designers of accounting systems should perhaps be concerned with transfer pricing procedures which maintain the philosophy of decentralization and which allow managers to take feasible actions. Systems which follow the principles of responsibility accounting, use market values and non-authoritative evaluation methods, may enhance learning. The proposal in this chapter is an attempt to indicate how this might be accomplished.

Whilst market values are most commonly perceived as some sort of solution to the transfer pricing problem, there is an equivalent for cost allocations. 'Stand alone' costs have been suggested as a way to introduce market verifiability into the allocation system and Troxels' article is useful in this respect.

Reference: Thomas, A.L. (1980b).

Further reading: Troxel, R.B. (1981) 'Corporate Cost Allocation can be Peaceful . . . . . Is Sharing the Key?' <u>Management Focus</u>, January-February, pp. 3-5.

2.   The strength of this statement depends on the effectiveness of governmental and fiscal interference and on whether international transfer pricing is seen as merely an extension of the domestic situation.

It is extremely difficult to gauge the effectiveness of present fiscal and host government rules. Transactions between related parties have and will continue to receive attention but the degree of influence depends on the efficacy of their rulings. Neither multinational companies nor the fiscal authorities are responding on this point for obvious reasons.

Empirical evidence comparing transfer pricing in the domestic and international settings is limited. However, the facts that international transfer prices can reduce global tax liability, mitigate the worst effects of currency fluctuations or ensure repatriation of dividends and profits adds extra dimensions which are not encountered in the domestic situation.

Reference: Plasschaert, S.R.F. (1979)

Further reading: Choi, F.D.S. and G.G. Mueller (1978) <u>An Introduction to</u> <u>Multinational Accounting</u>, Prentice Hall, Chapter 9.

3.   (a)

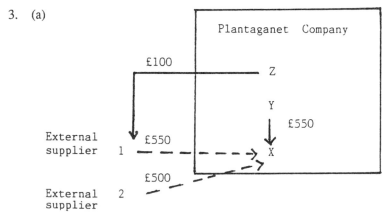

The interdependence between Division Y and X is sequential.

The interdependence between Division Z and X is indirectly sequential.

(b) From the company's view, the following costs relating to the alternative sources of the component are appropriate.

External Supplier 2	<u>£500</u>
External Supplier 1	£550
less contribution of Div. Z	<u>60</u>
	<u>£490</u>
Division Y	£550
less contribution of Div. Y	<u>200</u>
	<u>£350</u>

The company would prefer Division X to purchase from Division Y, that is, at the lowest incremental cost to the company. The astute student may argue that there is another alternative, that of Division Z supplying Y with the raw material. For this alternative, the incremental cost is £340 and should be preferred. This assumes that the raw material supplied by Z is the same as that purchased externally by Division Y.

(c) The company would favour an internal purchase. However the manager of Division X may prefer to place the order with external supplier 2 which results in the lowest cost for the division (£500 as opposed to £550). To support his case, this manager may argue that:

(i) he is not responsible for his division's profit unless he can choose the lowest bid as he sees it

(ii) he is entitled to test the external market in order to maintain divisional autonomy (iii)　if the external market gives imperfect values for the components, then divisions other than his own should adjust their prices to ensure that the internal trade takes place.

(d) It is apparent that the internal trade could take place at a transfer price in the range of £350 up to £500 (£340 — £500 if Division Z provides Y with the raw material). At a low transfer price, all or most of the profit will be credited to Division X. Division Y is working at full capacity and may justifiably argue that the opportunity cost of supplying X is not marginal or variable cost but the contribution forgone when supplying external customers, presumably at the price of £550. Division Y will want to maintain a contribution of £200 and even if the raw materials are bought from Z, the transfer price will still amount to £540. Division Z may be willing to provide the raw material at £40 to Y because Z has spare capacity but this is not certain. At a transfer price of £40, Z receives no contribution on the internal trade and Z may argue that a contribution of £60 is more appropriate, the price external supplier 1 is willing to pay.

It therefore appears unlikely that the divisions will be able to agree a transfer price to meet the external offer of £500 because each division is concerned with recording as favourable a financial performance measure as possible. Corporate management may dictate that the trade will take place internally but this may be divisive now and, in future the divisions may not provide accurate information about variable and incremental costs. Corporate management may state the method by which the transfer price is to be determined. Variable cost may be appropriate for Division Z but not for Division Y and the appropriate opportunity cost value will change with the market conditions for these divisions' outputs. Constant monitoring, adjustments and readjustments to the transfer price are necessitated at the corporate management level. Transfer prices based on methods which relate profit to divisional costs are likely to be seen as inequitable by at least one division. In the final analysis, it may be appropriate for the corporate management to adopt a 'hands-off' approach and recognise that decentralisation may result in sub-optimal decisions. The motivation of the divisional managers may be changed by less emphasis being placed on financial performance measures and evaluation over a longer time horizon.

Reference: Solomons, D. (1965)

Further reading: Emmanuel, C.R. (1977) 'Transfer Pricing: A Diagnosis and Possible Solution to Dysfunctional Decision-Making in the Divisionalised Company' <u>Management International Review</u>, No. 4, pp. 45-59.

4. (a) To charge or not to charge for the central computer services is the concern of this question. Allowing the service free of charge ensures that use is made of the computer by the audit teams. When there is no charge, audit teams may be more innovative in experimenting with applications of computer services. Conversely, the service may be mis-used on trivial, non-urgent matters.

A charge on the actual usage made of the computer services causes the audit teams to evaluate the benefits of computerized assistance versus the costs. Only those tried and tested applications which result in a saving will be undertaken. If the charge is inappropriately set, the central computer service may be underutilized and the proposed investment unjustified.

(b) Let's assume that each audit teams' actual usage is measured by lines of computer print-out. The central computer services unit may be able to provide accurate costs for increasing levels of usage. In contrast to the economist's marginal cost curve, this schedule may exhibit steps such as when the five extra staff and capital expenditure are incurred in order to exceed present output capacity. In the short-term, the user of 50 000 lines may be charged the same marginal cost as the user of 500 000 lines. However, in the longer-term, when a 'step' is encountered, additional users will be charged at the higher rate. Technically, an audit team may be charged at one marginal cost for 49 990 lines of output and at a higher rate for the last 10 lines. Alternatively, if one audit team abandons its use of the service, all other teams may benefit because the total usage now is below a marginal cost step. Hence marginal cost transfer prices in practice apply over restricted ranges and the decisions of other managers can adversely or beneficially affect the charge to the individual manager.

(c) Incremental cost saving appears to be a possible contender. Over a sustained period of time, the cost of operating the audit team with the computer service is compared to the cost without the computer service. However, this involves comparison with different periods of time and other factors may have subsequently changed. The audit team members are more or less experienced professionally and with the interpretation and application of computer print-outs, etc. Costs other than the computer service charge may have changed.

To monitor the effectiveness of the use of the computer service, perhaps the marginal cost transfer price could be compared with the cost of using an external computer bureau of equivalent quality and size. But this is more of a check on the computer service unit than the audit team. If the audit team's client revenues are compared with the costs of operating the audit team, including the marginal cost transfer price for computer services, significant variations may be detected. When the charge for computer services is a significant portion of total costs, the marginal cost transfer price may result in new clients being turned away or new clients being relatively sought. The former decisions may be conditioned by expectations that a 'step' is imminent and all other audit teams are maintaining their existing operations. The decision actively to pursue new clients may be conditioned by the view that all other audit teams are increasing their operations and no 'step' is in prospect.

A more telling comparison to evaluate audit team performance may be the number of clients requiring advice over a number of years; the number of hours engaged on client premises compared with previous years, etc. For the computer service, the number of actual lines of print-out over time and in comparison with expected use may indicate how responsive the audit team is to the marginal cost transfer pricing system.

Reference: Tomkins, C.R. (1973)

Further reading: Goetz, B.E. (1967) 'Transfer Prices: An Exercise in Relevancy and Goal Congruence' The Accounting Review, July, pp. 435-40.

5. (a)

	Revenue	**Manufacturing Cost (Cm)**	**Distribution Cost (Cd)**
Average	$205 - 0.5Q$	$19 + Q$	$10 + 0.7Q$
Total	$205Q - 0.5Q^2$	$19Q + Q^2$	$10Q + 0.7Q^2$
Marginal	$205 - Q$	$19 + 2Q$	$10 + 1.4Q$

Optimal output: $205 - Q = 19 + 2Q + 10 + 1.4Q$

$$Q = 40 \text{ units}$$

Transfer price associated with optimal output:

$$19 + 2Q = £99 \text{ per unit}$$

(b)

Manufacturing Division		Distribution Division		
Transfer price (£99x40)	3 960	Sales (205–20)40		7 400
Cm. (19+40)40	2 360	Transfer price	3960	
Profit	£1 600	Cd (10+28)40	1520	5 480
		Profit		£1 920

Baron Company profit = £3 520

(c) (i) **Supplier acting as internal monopolist**

In this instance it is to the supplying division's advantage to perceive the distributor's marginal data as average. Hence, the maximum the distributor is perceived to be willing to pay is as follows.

$205 - Q - (10 + 1.4Q)$ (perceived as average)

$205Q - Q^2 - (10Q + 1.4Q^2)$ (perceived as total)

$205 - 2Q - 10 - 2.8Q$ (perceived as marginal)

or $195 - 4.8Q$

Optimal output from supplier's view

$19 + 2Q = 195 - 4.8Q$

$Q = 25.88$ units

When this output level is incorporated with the correct net marginal revenue, the following transfer price is given.

$195 - 2.4Q = $ £132.89 per unit.

Manufacturing Division		Distribution Division		
Transfer price 132.89(25.88)	£3439.19	Revenue (205 – 12.94)25.88		£4970.50
Cm (19+25.88) 25.88	1161.49	Transfer price	3439.19	
	£2277.70	Cd(10+18.116)25.88	727.64	4166.82
Company profit = £3081.38				£ 803.68

132

By intentionally misinterpreting the data, the manufacturing division has been able to increase substantially its profit at the expense of the distribution division and to the detriment of the Baron Company overall.

(c) ii) **Distribution acting as internal monopsonist**

It will be to the distributor's advantage in this case to treat the marginal manufacturing cost as average cost data.

Hence,

$19 + 2Q$ (perceived as average)

$19Q + 2Q^2$ (perceived as total)

$19 + 4Q$ (perceived as marginal)

Optimal output from distributor's view point.

$205 - Q = 19 + 4Q + 10 + 1.4Q$

$Q = 27.5$ unit

When this output is incorporated in the correct marginal cost, the transfer price becomes:

$19 + 2(27.5) = £74$ per unit.

Manufacturing Division		Distribution Division		
Transfer price 74(27.5)	£2 035	Revenue (205-13.75)27.5		£5 259.38
Cm (19+27.5)27.5	1 278.75	Transfer price	2 035	
	£ 756.25	Cd(10+19.25)27.5	804.38	2 839.38
				£2 420

Company profit = £3176.25

Again, one division has benefited; distribution this time shows an apparent improvement in profit at the expense of manufacturing and overall company profit.

(d) (i) **Constant manufacturing cost**

$$\text{Optimal output:} \qquad 205 - Q = 99 + 10 + 1.4Q$$

$$Q = 40$$

Transfer price   £99 per unit

Manufacturer's profit is zero. Distributor's profit is £1920 which is also the Baron Company's total optimal profit in this case.

(d) (ii) **Declining manufacturing cost**

$$\text{Optimal output :} \qquad 205 - Q = 107 - 0.2Q + 10 + 1.4Q$$

$$Q = 40$$

Transfer price $= 107 - 0.2(40) = £99$ per unit.

Manufacturer's profit is £(160), distributor's profit is £1920 and the Baron Company's overall optimal profit is £1 760.

(e) The difference between cases (d) (i) and (ii) relates to the shape of the supplier's cost curve. Initially it is regarded as horizontal and hence gives no profit to this division. In the second instance, cost declines in a manner consistent with economies of scale. A loss is then recorded against this division. In the earlier parts of the question, the supplier's costs are assumed to increase with output and even when faced with monopsonistic pressure, (c) (ii), the supplying division still makes some profit. The astute manager may therefore forecast that rising costs are always in his interest, even to the extent of shifting the Cm curve upwards. Biasing of forecasted costs may be difficult to detect and standards for a variety of products may be equally problematic to set.

(f) Cases (c) (i) and (ii) indicate how one manager when given all the relevant and accurate information may still attempt to dominate another division for selfish reasons. Cases (d) (i), (ii) and (e) indicate the impact the shape of the cost curve has and how managers may be motivated to provide inaccurate information. Given these problems, the reasons for distinguishing the activities as separate divisions may be reappraised.

The strategic alternative of amalgamating the two divisions may be contemplated. This should be discussed in the wider context of the environments faced by the divisions now and in the future. The tactical alternative of reducing the emphasis on short-term profit measures may also be evaluated but this has implications for managerial status, motivation and performance evaluation. Finally, the use of a different form of transfer pricing may be considered (e.g. negotiated, two part tariff). However, all of the possibilities require an appreciation of how important integrating the divisions' activities are now and will be in the future, versus the intangible benefits associated with pseudo profit responsibility.

Reference: Thomas, A.L. (1980b)

Further reading: Onsi, M. (1970) 'A Transfer Pricing System Based on Opportunity

Cost' The Accounting Review, July, pp. 535-543.

6. The following diagram gives the salient points of the Birch Paper Company Case.

The Facts of the Birch Paper Company Case

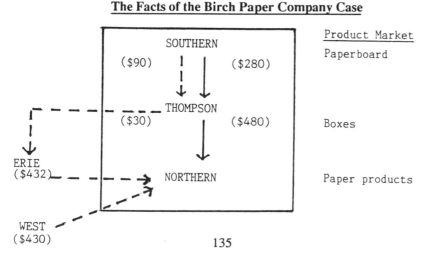

The incremental analysis given the facts in the case reveal the following from the Company's view:

West	$ 430
Erie	$ 432
less contribution to Southern 36	
less contribution to Thompson 5	41
	$ 391

Thompson	$ 480
less contribution to Southern 112	
less contribution to Thompson 80	192
	$ 288

Hence, Northern would prefer to buy from West at the lowest cost to the division whilst the company prefers the internal trade because this is the lowest cost to the company.

A resolution of this problem hinges on the Thompson Division's expectation that the market price will be closer to $480 than the $430 suggested by West. Hence, let Ms be $480, the market price expected by Thompson; Mb, the market price Northern is expecting, that is $430 and St, the standard variable cost of manufacture which from Thompson's view is $400 (Southern's transfer price and Thompson's variable cost). Then applying the maximum discount formula consistent with the fair and neutral transfer pricing procedure:

$$(1 - dtj\ max)\ Ms\ = 2\ St - Mb$$
$$(1 - dtj\ max)\ 480 = 2\ (400) - 430$$
$$dtj\ max = 23\%.$$

The lowest transfer price Thompson could offer is $370, [(0.77) 480]. With the application of the lost contribution charge providing an incentive, Thompson could match the Eire or West bids and still show a profit, even when Southern's transfer price remains at $280.

If the same procedure is applied to Southern, the following discount emerges:

$$(1 - dtj \ max) \ Ms = 2 \ St - Mb$$
$$(1 - dtj \ max) \ 280 = 2 \ (168) - 90 \ *$$
$$dtj \ max = 12\% \ approx.$$

*This figure is assumed to be the price Thompson believes Southern's output will command. It is the price associated with supplying Eire.

Again, with the application to be the lost contribution charge, Southern may be encouraged to supply Thompson at a transfer price as low as $246 approximately. In turn this would affect Thompson's perception of the variable costs of supplying Northern and will increase the range over which the transfer price can be negotiated. [With the minimum transfer price from Southern set at this level, Thompson could offer Northern a transfer price as low as $302.]

The divisional profit calculations cannot be undertaken without including hypothetical figures relating to the excess capacity at Southern and Thompson. However the example should serve the purpose of indicating how the proposal extends the range of potential transfer prices at the budget setting stage. The subsequent calculation of the period cost will clearly show which managers' anticipations were closer to reality. In the meantime, a decision to trade externally has not been taken on the basis of inappropriate accounting data.

Reference: Emmanuel, C.R. and Gee, K.P. (1982)

Further reading: Emmanuel, C.R. (1977), 'The Birch Paper Company: a Possible Solution to the Interdivisional Pricing Problem,' The Accountant's Magazine, May, pp. 195-198.

7. (a)

	Motor Pump Division	Engineering Division	
	Manufacturing cost	Distribution cost	Revenue
Average	$10 + 1.5Q$	$25 + 8.8Q$	$305 - 0.6Q$
Total	$10Q + 1.5Q^2$	$25Q + 8.8Q^2$	$305Q - 0.6Q^2$
Marginal	$10 + 3Q$	$25 + 17.6Q$	$305 - 1.2Q$

Optimal quantity   MC = MR

$$10 + 3Q + 25 + 17.6Q \ = \ 305 - 1.2Q$$
$$21.8Q \ = \ 270$$
$$Q \ = \ 12.385 \text{ batches}$$
$$\text{or } 1\ 238.5 \text{ motor pumps}$$

Optimal transfer price $10 + 3(12.385)$ = £47.155 per batch

Profit Statement: Motor Pump Division

Revenue (47.155 x 12.385)	584
Manufacturing [$10(12.385)+(1.5(12.385)^2$]	353.85
Profit	230.15

Engineering Division

Revenue [$305(12.385)+8.8(12.385)^2$]		3 685.43
Transfer Price	584	
Distribution cost [$25(12.385)+8.8(12.385)^2$]	1 659.45	2 243.45
Profit		1 441.98

Check: Corporate Profit

Revenue [305(12.385)–0.6(12.385)^2]		3 685.43
Manufacturing [10(12.385)+1.5(12.385)^2]	353.85	
Distribution [25(12.385)+8.8(12.385)^2]	1659.45	2 013.30
Profit		1 672.13

(b) External quotations below the Pump division's required transfer price of £180 are available. However, the analysis in (a) suggests that a transfer price as low as £47 per batch still allows the pump division a margin of profit. If Engineering buys externally at £160 per batch, the company will lose £27 per batch [160–(180–47)]. Whether this is sufficiently significant for top management to intervene depends on:

(i)   The commitment to a 'hands-off' decentralised management control system.

(ii)   Whether the pump division will be able to sell externally at £180 per batch.

(iii)   Whether the independent suppliers are distress pricing for tactical reasons.

(iv)   Whether the quality, delivery times, etc of the external suppliers are equivalent to the pump division.

(c) The information provided by the divisions must be accurate and honest. Given that divisional managers know how the information will be used, manipulation cannot be ruled out. For example, the pump division by creating an upward shift in the manufacturing cost function can ensure a higher transfer price. Likewise the engineering division may under-estimate the revenue function to obtain a lower transfer price.

In fact, the supplying division will not be able to show a profit unless its cost function is upward sloping. There is an incentive to include diseconomies of scale or extra costs to achieve this. Top management may only be able to check the reliability of the cost and revenue function after incurring considerable monitoring costs which, in themselves, are contrary to the philosophy of decentralization.

(d) In all but one set of circumstances the transfer pricing problem may be regarded as a subset of the allocation problem. That is, whatever the transfer price, corporate profit is unaffected.

When divisional managers have clear discretion to trade externally; when the external market trades in commodities, components, services etc which are largely indistinguishable from those available internally and when divisional managers are not required to transmit information to the centre or top management; in these circumstances the transfer price can affect total corporate profits as well as reported divisional profits.

Reference: Gould (1964) 'Internal Pricing in Firms when there are costs of using an outside market' Journal of Business, Vol 37, pp 61-67).

8.   (a) **Earlswood**

	Revenue	**Manufacturing**	**Distribution**
Average cost per unit	$350 - 0.8Q$	$28 + 2Q$	$14 + 0.7Q$
Total cost per unit	$350Q - 0.8Q^2$	$28Q + 2Q^2$	$14Q + 0.7Q^2$
Marginal cost per unit	$350 - 1.6Q$	$28 + 4Q$	$14 + 1.4Q$

Optimal Output

$$350 - 1.6Q = 28 + 4Q + 14 + 1.4Q$$

$$Q = 44$$

Transfer price associated with optimal output

$$28 + 4(44) = £204$$

(b)

Square Division		Knight Division	
Transfer price	£	Revenue	£
(204)44	8 976	$350(44) - 0.8(44)^2$	13 851.2
Manufacturing costs		Distribution costs	
$(28)44 + 2(44)^2$	5 104	$14(44) + 0.7(44)^2$	1 971.2
		Transfer Price	8 976
	3 872		2 904

(c) The application of the economist's marginal analysis requires

(i) Information about cost and revenue schedules which is treated as certain and the information is presumed to be given honestly. Unfortunately, the Square Division could increase the transfer price by biasing the manufacturing cost schedule upwards; Knight Division by biasing the revenue estimate downwards. Due to information asymmetry, neither practice may be easily detected.

(ii) A corporate policy which ensures that internal demand is first met or internal supply is first sought in order to be efficient. When an intermediate external market exists, it is likely to be highly imperfect and not a single but a range of market prices will be available. The use of a 'captive' market policy adversely affects the divisional managers' autonomy and hence, their feelings of responsibility for profit performance.

(iii) The corporate management, headquarters staff or one of the divisional managers to process the information and generate the optimal transfer price. Even the iterative procedure of the decomposition LP approach requires someone in the organization to call a halt to the deliberations. The perceptions of divisional managers may be that the setting of the transfer price is outside their control and they are merely decision executors not decision makers.

(d) Other methods may include transfer prices based on: standard or actual variable cost; standard or actual full costs; standard or actual full costs plus a profit percentage, etc. Or methods such as Solomons two part tariff or Emmanuel and Gee's fair and neutral procedure. All have limitations with the possible exception of the latter.

Reference: Grabski S V (1985) 'Transfer Pricing in Comple Organizations: A Review and Integration of Recent Empirical and Analytical Research' Journal of Accounting Literature, Vol 4, pp 33-75.)

CHAPTER 12

THE CAPITAL INVESTMENT DECISION IN THE MULTIDIVISIONAL COMPANY

1. The stages of the capital budgeting process are:

   (a) project generation or origination

   (b) estimation of cash flows

   (c) progress through the organization

   (d) analysis and selection of projects

   (e) authorization of expenditure

   (f) post-audit investigation

   In multidivisional companies each stage may be formally recognized whereas in business organizations which are smaller in size of scale of operation, the stages may be part of an informal, sub-conscious capital budgeting process used by the owner-managers.

   Problems associated with the accuracy and the completeness of the information entering the capital budgeting process are likely to be most prevalent in stages (a)-(c).

   (a) Lower level managers will not submit projects which may reduce current operating performance as measured by accrual income.

   (b) Projects which improve current operating performance in the short term may be submitted in preference to competing projects which yield a higher NPV.

   (c) Cash flow estimates especially for the later years of the project's life may be biased to ensure acceptance at a given discount rate.

143

(d) Political pressure, returning favours and parochial interests may be used to gather support for a 'second-best' project.

Top management must recognize the existence of information assymetry and lower level managers' ability to influence the first three stages of the process especially. To remove some of the motivation to provide inaccurate and incomplete information about project proposals, top management may:

(a) re-appraise the use of short-term financial performance measures to reward managers

(b) provide the assumptions underlying strategic plans and allow lower level managers to comment on the profile that the plan envisages for their part of the business,

(c) provide guidelines about macro-economics such as national inflation forecasts or trade journal forecasts to help in estimating cash flows.

Reference: King, P. (1975)

Further reading: Pinches, G.E. (1982) 'Myopia, capital budgeting and decision-making'. Financial Management, Autumn, pp. 6-19.

2. (a) **FOR:**

(i) The 'supremo' may ensure that all projects follow standard practice of presentation.

(ii) The 'supremo' may ensure that all projects follow the same assumptions about GNP growth, inflation etc.

AGAINST:

(i) Monitoring costs are increased by the creation of the new position.

(ii) Dependent on the way in which the checking is done (supportive or recriminatory), fewer projects may be generated.

144

(b) **FOR:**

(i)   Greater standardization of accounting practices may result.

(ii)   No extra cost is apparently associated with this alternative.

AGAINST:

(i)   Attention to generally accepted accounting principles may dominate considerations of commercial, economic or environmental forecasts of key variables.

(ii)   Divisional accountants may be seen as watchdogs for top management and not as members of the divisional management team.

(c) **FOR:**

(i)   Expertise in forecasting and knowledge of particular industrial or product-market trends may complement the divisional manager's experience to provide more realistic cash flow estimates.

(ii)   The head office team may be able to improve or up-date the divisional manager's predictive model.

AGAINST:

(i)   The advice comes too late in that competing projects have already been considered and rejected by the divisional managers.

(ii)   The 'advice' may be viewed as undermining the divisional manager's autonomy and authority.

(d) **FOR:**

(i)   This may result in a greater number of projects being proposed and submitted to the capital budgeting process.

(ii)   Projects which contribute to a strategic plan or profile envisaged by the divisional manager may be freely submitted even though under DCF they would have been rejected. It may encourage proposals which involve inter-divisional trading to be forthcoming.

(iii)   The motivation to bias cash flow estimates is reduced.

AGAINST:

(i)   The selection of projects may appear haphazard with different criteria being used to define "merits" for different projects at different times.

(ii)   The continued reliance on short-term accruals income to measure divisional performance may encourage short-lived projects which improve the accounting measure regardless of DCF considerations.

(iii)   Opportunistic behaviour by divisional managers is unfettered and a motive to bias the generation of projects and the estimate of cash flows is provided by the evaluation style.

Reference: Scapens, R.W. et al (1982)

Further reading: Heebink, D.V. (1964) 'The Optimum Capital Budget', The Accounting Review, January, pp. 90-93.

3.   **Residual Income**

Advantages

(a) Managerial and divisional performance are distinguished – controllable RI and net RI respectively.

(b) Controllability and hence responsibility are the underlying concepts governing measurement.

(c) Controllable RI is an absolute number and hence provides less scope for the manager of an investment centre to manipulate results.

(d) Under certain conditions (viz. constant cash flow, annuity depreciation, the hurdle rate being equivalent to the cost of capital), RI is the short-run counterpart of net present value.

Disadvantages

(a) Controllable investment is difficult to gauge in practice.

(b) The interest charge on controllable investment is difficult to uphold as an opportunity cost because the company and/or divisional cost of capital cannot be accurately calculated.

(c) Inter-divisional comparisons of RI are dangerous because there is a built-in advantage favouring larger divisions.

(d) Non-constant cash flows require each year's RI to be calculated and discounted in order to be equivalent to net present value which may not conform with the short time horizon of divisional managers.

Rate of Return on Investment

Advantages

(a) It is a well-accepted measure of performance which can be calculated in accordance with the concept of controllability.

(b) Inter-divisional comparisons using ROI may be informative if consistent accounting practices are employed throughout the firm.

(c) ROI is consistent with IRR (internal rate of return) if annuity depreciation at the IRR discount rate is used and cash flows are constant.

(d) ROI provides the same target for a manager to aim for in absolute profit terms if the manager cannot influence the investment base.

Disadvantages

(a) Controllable investment is difficult to gauge in practice.

(b) ROI being a rate allows the divisional manager to manipulate costs, revenues and investments to attain (or over-attain) a target set by this means.

(c) Divisional managers may be unwilling to propose capital projects which reduce the current ROI but which nevertheless have an acceptable NPV or IRR from the company's view.

(d) The equivalence of ROI with annuity depreciation and IRR will not occur, except by coincidence, when cash flows follow an unconventional pattern.

Integrated Contribution Budget

Advantages

(a) The integrated contribution budget is consistent with the responsibility of an investment centre manager or, with the exclusion of the capital budget, is consistent with profit centre responsibility.

(b) All inputs to the budget are in cash flow terms and allow the assumptions of the capital budget to be matched with those of the fixed/managed and contribution budgets.

(c) Cash flow accounting avoids the allocation problems caused by depreciation, etc. which are embedded in all accruals income measures like ROI and RI.

(d) It is a closer approximation of economic income and hence improves the compatability of short-term and long-term decision-making.

Disadvantages

(a) Reconciling cash flow performance with accruals income required by external financial reporting is problematic. Perhaps external users would prefer cash flow reports!

(b) Cash flow accountIng is conceptually difficult to link with any known transfer pricing practices.

(c) Cash flow is only an approximation of opportunity cost and hence, the consistency with economic income may be justifiably questioned.

(d) The need to revise cash flow estimates in the capital budget on the grounds of changed assumptions may result in cumbersome revisions affecting the integrated contribution budget.

Reference: Tomkins, C.R. (1973)

Further reading: Mepham, M.J. (1980) 'The residual income debate' <u>Journal of Business Finance and Accounting</u>, Summer, pp. 183-199.

4.   There is no guarantee that an integrated cash flow AIS will prevent opportunistic behaviour by divisional managers. The original budget estimates may be provided by the divisional manager to create slack targets in order to obtain any rewards associated with a favourable actual-budgeted comparison. If the divisional manager's participation is constrained, the timing of cash payments or receipts may be manipulated to give an appearance of improvement in the actual results.

However, in the first case, the provision of assumptions to substantiate the cash flow estimates in the different budgets allows a check on the consistency of the assumptions to be made, both now and in the future. In the second case, the timing of receipts and payments can be verified albeit at increased monitoring costs.

As with all AIS, the integrated cash flow proposal needs to be evaluated in the context of overall management control which the business enterprise believes is appropriate. The main advantage of the proposal appears to lie in the fact that the same cash flows used in the long-term investment decision are fed into the contribution budget at the appropriate time. Hence, the motivation to bias estimates may be reduced because future operating performance will depend on the realism of these estimates. When divisional managers have this level of participation, it is essential that the AIS does not misdirect the manager's decision-making to attain short-term financial performance measures expressed in a different form to those in the planning model. It is also necessary that additional measures of managerial effort are reported and that a comparison of the assumptions and actual outcomes is made to determine the validity of the manager's predictive model.

Such a comparison requires top management to be supportive and helpful. Attaching blame to the divisional manager for inaccurately identifying key variables or assumptions is likely to lead to future plans being based on key variables over which the manager has little or no control or on bland, non-specific assumptions. By means of democratic interaction and a de-emphasis on any short-term measures of performance, the divisional managers may recognize that the integrated cash flow AIS promotes self-control and learning. The fact that long-term planning and short-term operating decisions are in the same terms (viz. cash flows) reveals more clearly their interaction and interdependence. Although opportunistic behaviour cannot be eliminated by any AIS, the provision of true participation, useful feedback on financial information and key variable assumptions, and a supportive, long-term style of evaluation may contribute to reduce the motivation to make intentionally self-interested decisions.

Reference: Henderson, B.D. and Dearden D. (1966)

Further reading: Larcker, D.F. (1981) 'The perceived importance of selected information characteristics for strategic capital budgeting decisions', The Accounting Review, July, pp. 519-538.

5. (a)

	YEAR 1	2	3	4	5
Asset value at year beginning	£1500K	1200K	900K	600K	300K
Net cash flow	400	400	400	400	400
Depreciation	300	300	300	300	300
Net Profit	100	100	100	100	100
Interest on capital	150	120	90	60	30
RI	(50)	(20)	10	40	70
ROI	6.7%	8.3%	11.1%	16.7%	33.3%

(b) RI with annuity depreciation

$$1500K - a\,\overline{5}|.10 = £395.7K$$

	YEAR 1	2	3	4	5
Asset value at year beginning	1500K	1254.3K	984K	686.7K	359.7K
Net cash inflow	400	400	400	400	400
Depreciation	245.7	270.3	297.3	327.0	359.7
Interest on capital	150	125.4	98.4	68.7	36.0
	395.7	395.7	395.7	395.7	395.7
	4.3	4.3	4.3	4.3	4.3

Discounting the RI stream $4.3K \div a\,\overline{5}|\,.1 = £16\,300$

151

which is equivalent (subject to rounding errors) to the net present value

$$\text{NPV} \quad = \quad -1500\text{K} + 400 \, a \, \overline{5}|.1$$
$$= \quad \underline{\text{£16 320}}$$

(c) **Advantages**

(i)   RI is equivalent to NPV when the individual annual results calculated using annuity depreciation are discounted at the same rate used in the capital investment decision.

(ii)   When the cash flows are constant, the divisional manager needs only to consult the first year's RI result to discover whether the project is worth proposing.

(iii)   Hence the manager should be favourably disposed to submitting any project which gives positive earnings in excess of the company's cost of capital and will not be misdirected to improve the current ROI when it is greater than the company's cost of capital.

Disadvantages

(i)   The use of annuity depreciation is unlikely to be found acceptable in practice.   As opposed to all other methods, this depreciation charge increases as the project ages.

(ii)   In order to have separate measures of managerial and divisional performance, controllable and non-controllable investments need to be distinguished and this is not easy to achieve in practice.

(iii)   The interest charge may be based on the company's or the divisional cost of capital. Both alternatives are difficult to calculate.

Hence, RI may be argued to be theoretically superior to ROI but RI has certain technical disadvantages in its application.

152

Further reading: Beraneks, W. (1984) 'A Note on the Equivalence of Certain Capital Budgeting, criteria', The Accounting Review, October, pp. 914-916.

6. (a) A comparison of NPV and net realizable value (NRV) reveals that the company would not wish the asset sold.

NPV > NRV (33 657 – 30 000 = £3 657)

(b)

HOLD ASSET	Year 1	2	3	4	5
Asset balance at year beginning	50 000	45 000	40 000	35 000	30 000
Net cash flow	7 000	7 000	7 000	7 000	7 000
Depreciation	5 000	5 000	5 000	5 000	5 000
Interest on capital	5 000	4 500	4 000	3 500	3 000
RI	(3 000)	(2 500)	(2 000)	(1 500)	(1 000)

If JPR Williams sells the asset, his current year RI will sustain a book loss of £20 000 (£50 000 – 30 000).

The divisional manager may prefer the smaller loss associated with holding the asset rather than selling it.

(c) Having recently been appointed, the divisional manager may prefer to sell the asset now thereby eliminating the pattern of negative RIs which continue over the full ten year life of the asset.

(d) With a saleable value of £35 000, the company would favour disposing of the asset now.

The RI results associated with holding the asset would not change but the book loss of selling would reduce to £15 000. Hence the divisional manager may still prefer to hold the asset.

Under the original circumstances, the company and divisional view result in the same decision being preferred, i.e. hold the asset. The fact that this equivalence is purely coincidental is illustrated when the saleable value becomes £35 000. Now the company view is to sell the asset while the manager may still prefer to hold it.

RI with conventional methods of depreciation will only coincidentally give a decision consistent with NPV. The information in the control model (RI) is different from that in the planning model (NPV).

Reference: Amey, L.R. and D.A. Egginton (1973)

Further reading: Wright, F.K. (1962), 'Measuring Project Profitability: Rate of Return or Present Value', The Accounting Review, July, pp. 433-437.

7.

	PLANT X			PLANT Y		
	ACTUAL	**EXPECTED**	**VARIANCE**	**ACTUAL**	**EXPECTED**	**VARIANCE**
YEAR 2						
Net cash						
flow	£80 000	100 000	(20 000)	£105 000	100 000	5 000
Depreciation	60 000	60 000		80 000	80 000	
Interest on						
capital	19 200*	19 200		25 600	25 600	
RI	800	20 800	(20 000)	(600)	(5 600)	5 000

* Calculated on year beginning balances i.e.

plant X 0.08 (240 000) = 19 200

plant Y 0.08 (320 000) = 25 600

Assumptions Appraising Performance

The table shows that a variance of the same strength and direction is recorded whether the RI of the individual plant is examined or the net cash flows. Under these circumstances, the merits of RI budgeted and actual comparisons over comparisons of budgeted and actual net cash flows or even net profit may be questioned. It is generally assumed that the RI measure more accurately reflects the degree of control exercised by the plant manager.

The adverse variance at plant X is due to the down-turn in demand resulting from a competitor's innovation. The computation above assumes that the plant manager failed to foresee this event for which he is responsible. Alternatively, if he is not held responsible and his estimate of £25 000 lost cash flow is accepted, his second year performance report becomes:

PLANT X

	Actual	Expected	Variance
Net cash flow	£105 000	100 000	5 000
Depreciaton	60 000	60 000	
Interest on capital	19 200	19 200	
	25 800	20 800	5 000

The comparison of net cash flow gives the same result as the RI comparison.

In the case of plant Y, the favourable variance is totally due to the unexpected sale of skate-board wheels to a third party for £10 000. The inclusion of this amount is only merited if the manager was responsible for developing this market. If he was not, then the actual net cash flow should be reduced by £10 000 or the targeted net cash flow should be increased by £10 000. An adverse variance of £5 000 is the result in either case. These alternatives cannot be made when the plant manager of Y is instrumental in finding the buyer and arranging the sale.

155

Plant Manager Performance

The important question to focus on here is whether plant managers of the same company should inform each other of external transactions which could affect the individual performance of the plants.

From the facts in the case, it is debatable whether the manager of plant Y should be held responsible for the reduction of £20 000 cash flow at X even if he did not tell X of the external sale and was aware of the purpose to which the skate-board wheels would be put. Y's commercial integrity would be in jeopardy and, should the information have prompted X to follow the innovation, a legal action by the external third party may be brought. If he was not informed of the external sale in advance, it appears difficult to hold the manager of X responsible for this.

Alternatively, if Y had approached X with the information and X has declined to act, the responsibility of the respective managers would be as originally shown.

These observations are subject to alternative interpretations.

A good answer should highlight:

(a) The cost of employing a sophisticated performance technique (RI) as opposed to a cash flow comparison.

(b) The difficulties in practice of presenting performance reports which accurately reflect the responsibilities of individual managers and the economic effects of the decisions they have taken.

Further reading: Peasnell, K.V. (1981) 'On Capital Budgeting and Income Measurement', Abacus, June, pp. 52-67.

8. (a) Machine I

Costs $800K + 247 a\overline{4}|.1 = 1\,582.96$

Minimum annual sales revenue $= 1582.96 \times \dfrac{1}{a\,\overline{4}|1} = \underline{£499.4K}$

Machine II

Costs $800K + 100V_{.1}{}^1 + 200V_{.1}{}^2 + 340V_{.1}{}^3 + 400V_{.1}{}^4$

$$= 1,584.83$$

Minimum annual sales revenue $= 1584.83 \times \dfrac{1}{a\,\overline{4}|.1} = \underline{£500K}$

(b)

Machine I	**Year 1**	**2**	**3**	**4**
Asset balance at year beginning	£800K	£600K	£400K	£200K
Cash inflow	499	499	499	499
Cash outflow	247	247	247	247
	252	252	252	252
Depreciation	200	200	200	200
Net profit	52	52	52	52
Interest on capital	80	60	40	20
RI	(28)	(8)	12	32
ROI	6.5%	8.7%	13%	26%

Machine II	Year 1	2	3	4
Asset balance at year beginning	£800K	£600K	£400K	£200K
Cash inflow	500	500	500	500
Cash outflow	100	200	340	400
	400	300	160	100
Depreciation	200	200	200	200
Net profit	200	100	(40)	(100)
Interest on capital	80	60	40	20
RI	120	40	(80)	(120)
ROI	25%	16.7%	(10%)	(50%)

(c) Annuity depreciation for both machines

$$800K - a\,\overline{4}|.1 = £252.37K$$

rounded to £252K.

Machine I	Year 1	2	3	4
Asset balance at year beginning	£800K	£628K	£439K	£231K
Cash inflow	499	499	499	499
Cash outflow	247	247	247	247
	252	252	252	252
Depreciation	172	189	208	229*
Net profit	80	63	44	23
Interest on capital	80	63	44	23
RI	-	-	-	-
ROI	10%	10%	10%	10%

* Due to rounding, the last year's depreciation is £2000 below the asset balance at year beginning.

Machine II	Year 1	2	3	4
Asset balance at year beginning	£800K	£628K	£439K	£231K
Cash inflow	500	500	500	500
Cash outflow	100	200	340	400
	400	300	160	100
Depreciation	172	189	208	229 *
Net profit	228	111	(48)	(129)
Interest on capital	80	63	44	23
RI	148	48	(92)	(152)
ROI	28.5%	17.6%	(11%)	(55.8%)

* Due to rounding there is an error of £2 000 in the underprovision for depreciation.

(d) As part (a) shows, both machines are marginal investments; the discounted net cash flows merely cover the initial cost of investment at 10%.

However, performance reports using historical cost depreciation and either RI or ROI measures do not indicate this marginality. For the ambitious manager, machine II may be preferred.

When annuity depreciation is employed, the RI and ROI performance measures reflect the true decision for machine I. However this is only due to the constant cash flows associated with this machine. The ambitious manager may still prefer machine II and it is only by discounting the annual RIs that the zero net present value can be gauged.

Reference: Scapens, R.W. (1978).

Further reading: Ferrara, W.L. (1977) 'Probabilistic Approaches to Return on Investment and Residual Income', The Accounting Review, July, pp. 597-604.

9. (a)

	Electrolysis	Ergometer
ROI GBV	12.1%	12.8%
ROI NBV	24.2%	25.6%
RI GBV	£8 000	£7 000
RI NBV	£27 000	£19 500

The manager of the electrolysis division chose RI and the manager of ergometer chose ROI.

On the limited data available, it is impossible to award the bonus. It is essential to learn what was expected, that is, a comparison with budgeted ROI, budgeted RI is needed.

(b)

(i) I_0 £30,000   Net cash inflow $t_1 - t_{10}$ £4000

Company view $-30\ 000 + 4000\ a_{\overline{10}|.10}$

= (5 421.6)

Electrolysis view: RI of project $4000 - 3000 = £1000$

This should ensure adoption by the divisional manager because it is a positive RI.

Ergometer division: ROI of project GBV 13.3%

NBV   13.3% minimum

t_6 26.6%

If evaluated by means of ROI on gross book value, the divisional manager may adopt the project although it is only a marginal improvement on the current performance. If evaluated on ROI, net book value, the manager will have to wait until the sixth year before the project improves the current level of performance.

Consistency with the corporate view will occur only coincidentally under either set of circumstances. The long-term planning model uses different data, essentially depreciation methods, to the short-term financial performance measures.

(ii) RI (and for that matter ROI) can be made consistent with the DCF model's results if annuity depreciation is employed where the discount rate is the same as the hurdle rate under the DCF calculation. If the cash flows follow an annuity, only the first year's RI (or ROI) results need to be examined but if this is not the case, the project's RI (or ROI) over its entire life needs to be determined and discounted to be equivalent to the net present value.

$$\frac{30\ 000 - a_{\overline{10}|.10}}{} = 4882.336 \text{ annuity depreciation}$$

$$RI = (\pounds 882)$$

(c) It is important because a lack of coincidence may result in projects which the company would adopt not being submitted by the divisional manager or the divisional manager submitting projects which although they meet the corporate criterion are second best because they give higher short-term pereformance measures at the expense of a lower NPV.

The submission or non-submission of capital projects to the formal capital budgeting process appears to be within the control of investment centre managers (King, Marsh, etc). Together with project generation, the investment centre manager may significantly influence or control the estimates of cash flow and the project's process of acceptance through the organization.

Given this influence, it seems essential that the short-term performance measure used to evaluate the manager and the division should accord with the long-term planning model utilising DCF techniques.

10. (a)

ROI

t_1 $23 - 16 \div 100 = 7\%$

t_2 $23 - 16 \div 84 = 8.3$

t_3 $7 \div 68 = 10.3$

t_4 $7 \div 52 = 13.5$

t_5 $7 \div 36 = 19.4$

t_6 $7 \div 20 = 35$

The effect in the first 4 years is to reduce Ozark's overall ROI, currently at 15%

RI

t_1 $23 - 16 \div 10 = (3)$

t_2 $7 \div 8.4 = (1.4)$

t_3 $7 \div 6.8 = 0.2$

t_4 $7 \div 5.2 = 1.8$

t_5 $7 \div 36 = 3.4$

t_6 $7 \div 2 = 5$

Given the adverse effect on RI in the first 2 years, it is unclear whether the project would be accepted by the Ozark Division.

Corporate view

$-100\ 000 + 23\ 000\ a^{\overline{6}}|1 + 4000\ v^6 1$

$-100\ 000 + 100\ 165 + 2256$

$= £2\ 421\ +\text{ve}$

(b) RI and Annuity

$$\text{Annuity Depreciatio} = \frac{I_0 - \text{Scrap Value}}{\overline{a_6}|7.1}$$

$$= \frac{100\,000 - 2256}{4.355}$$

$$= 22\,444$$

	Net Income	Cost of Capital	Depreciation	RI	Asset y/beg
t_1	23 000	10 000	12 444	556	100 000
t_2	23 000	8 756	13 688	556	87 556
t_3	23 000	7 387	15 057	556	73 868
t_4	23 000	5 881	16 563	556	58 811
t_5	23 000	4 225	18 219	556	42 248
t_6	23 000	2 403	20 041	556	24 029

Asset value at end of year 6 = 3988 – 4000 Scrap

£12 due to rounding

PV of RI = 2421.38 $(556\ \overline{a_6}|.1)$ which is consistent with NPV

Project may now be accepted because any positive RI will increase the short term, overall RI performance measure. For this to occur

(i)   annuity depreciation must be applied

(ii) with a rate consistent with the hurdle rate under NPV

(iii) there must be a constant cash flow in order that the manager reaches a congruent decision if only one or two years' analysis of the project is conducted.

163

(c) Lease payment as a proportion of annual cash inflow

$$\frac{I}{PV} = \frac{100\,000}{100\,165} = 0.9983$$

Lease payment $23\,000(0.9983) = 22\,962$

Annual Divisional Performance

Net cash inflow	23 000
Lease payment	22 962
Divisional income	38

$$\text{NPV} = 38\,a_{\overline{6}|}.\,1 + 4000\,V_{.1}6$$
$$= £2\,421$$

(d) The lack of consistency between the short-term accruals income performance measures and the long-term DCF decision models may misdirect divisional managers to

(i)   not submit capital projects the company would wish to accept

(ii)   submit projects which are second best, i.e. to improve the short-term measure but give a lower albeit positive NPV.

This can occur when divisional managers have significant influence over the origination of projects, the estimation of future cash flows and control over progress through the organization.

(e) Advantages of the contribution budget are:

(i)   only cash flows are included, hence eliminating allocation and historical cost

(ii)   consistency with the long-term decision models, eg NPV

(iii)   versatility with respect to profit, investment, revenue/cost centre management

(iv)   understanding of financial statements and budgets improved.

Disadvantages include

(i)   the value to be placed on transfer prices

(ii)   manipulation of cash flow data

(iii)   lack of consistency with financial reports prepared for external users

(iv)   introduction of confusion between economic value and accounting profit

(Ref: Marsh et al (1988) 'Managing Strategic Investment Decisions in Large Diversified Companies' in Pettigrew A.M. (ed) Competitiveness and the Management Process, Basil Blackwell.)

11. (a) Divisionalization can be in response to many factors, most of these factors relate to uncertainty. The creation of profit responsible units may occur due to growth in size, diversity of markets, products, geographical locations served, the need to shorten internal communication channels and improve swift reaction to market changes, etc. The conscious delegation of decision-making to lower level managers requires active support from the CEO or top management group, and must be consistent with their management style.

(b) Profit responsible decentralization requires:

(i)   that all costs and revenues can be traced to the divisional manager who is responsible for them.

(ii)   that no action will be taken that increases divisional profits at the expense of company profit.

(iii)   that managerial decisions and efficiency taken elsewhere in the company will not affect a separate division's performance.

(c) NPV

$-60\,000 + 15\,500\,(2)\,v^1._2 + 18\,600\,(2)\,v^2._2 + 19\,600\,(2)\,v^3._2 - 620\,\overline{a_3}|_2$

$-60\,000 + 25\,823 + 25\,817 + 22\,697 - 1\,306$

13 031 +ve

On the financial data available, the company would accept the project.

ROI

	t_1	t_2	t_3
Cash flow	30 380	36 580	38 580
Depreciation	20 000	20 000	20 000
Net Income	10 380	16 580	18 580
Investment at y/beg	60 000	40 000	20 000
ROI	17.3%	41.4%	92.9%

With a current ROI of 30%, James may be inclined to present this investment. It will depend on how long he expects to be in his present job.

RI with Annuity Depreciation

$60\ 000 - a_{\overline{3}|\ .2} = 28\ 490$

	t_1	t_2	t_3
Cash flow	30 380	36 580	38 580
Interest on			
Capital 12 000	8 702	4 784	
Depreciation 16 490	28 490 19 788 28 490	23 706 28 490	
	1 890	8 090	10 090
Balance at y/beg	60 000	43 150	23 722

$[NPV = 1\ 890\ (.833) + 8090\ (.694) + 10\ 090\ (.579)$

$= 13\ 031]$

NPV is equivalent with RI if

(i)   annuity depreciation is used

(ii)   the interest charge is the same as the cost of capital used in the NPV and annuity depreciation computation

(iii)   The first year's RI is only a good approximation of NPV when the project has constant cash flows.

Alternatively, the investment centre manager may be treated as having leased the divisional assets (Gregory, 1987).

Lease payment as a proportion of annual cash inflow:

$$\frac{I}{PV} = \frac{60\,000}{73\,031} = 0.82157$$

	t_1	t_2	t_3
Annual net cash inflows	30 380	36 580	38 580
Lease payments @ 0.82157	24 959	30 053	31 696
Divisional Income	5 421	6 527	6 884
Discounted @ 20%	4 516	4 530	3 986 = £13 032
			NPV

(Ref: Gregory A 'Divisional Performance Measurement with Divisions as Lessees of Head Office Assets' Accounting and Business Research, Summer (1987).

167

CHAPTER 13

ACCOUNTING FOR MANAGEMENT CONTROL

1. Figure 13.5 in the text may form a useful starting point to answer these questions.

(a) The motive for the inaccurate recording of material to individual jobs needs to be discovered. At the aggregate level, the budgeted and actual amounts appear to be consistent but for individual jobs, the manager seems to be recording material not actually used and not recording material that was used. The explanation for this behaviour may lie with the planning procedure.

If the manager records the material actually used accurately to each job and completes the job, he may still have to explain why the planned and actual usage are different. If he records accurately and the job remains incomplete at a certain time, he has to explain why the planned amount of material was not used and why the plan was not followed. If he records the amounts inaccurately and the job is completed on time, no explanation will be needed. If he records inaccurately and the job is incomplete at the appointed time, he can still show that the material used follows the plan. Hence, the lowest risk to the manager's well-being is associated with the inaccurate recording of material to individual jobs. This behaviour may be reinforced when the manager is evaluated by mean of short-term actual and budget comparisons. The main cause may be traced to the manager's lack of participation in planning. Without participation, the formal plans are of little use and the AIS does not indicate this when actual amounts are misrecorded to coincide with budget expectations.

(b) This case illustrates diffused responsibility. Each design section manager has responsibility for an individual component part but only ill-defined or negligible responsibility for the entire aircraft. A manager is unlikely to lose his job if the component is slightly overweight and works but if he tries a new design and it fails, it can be traced back to him.

This type of problem is likely to be encountered in functionally organized companies when the integration and coordination of activities has a high priority. Emphasizing individual sections' or departments' contributions and reporting upon them may be counter-productive especially when the measurement of output is confined to a single dimension such as whether the component works or fails.

To mitigate diffused responsibility is no easy matter but recording the output of the total collaborative effort, that is concentrating on the aircraft may help. Also attempting to measure the innovativeness of the individual design sections may alter some manager's attitudes. By recording contributions to professional or technical design journals, presentations at learned conferences or even the number of hours each design section has used wind-tunnels etc. may reflect more accurately the effort managers are making to design new, safe components.

(c) This is an example of deferred responsibility. The project chief is responding to what can be measured and hence recorded under the AIS. Meeting the production schedule and expected output level can be unambiguously evaluated whereas meeting quality control specifications is less easy to measure. Also, any defects in the micro-computer will not become known until customers begin to complain and start returning them. By that time the project chief may have moved on within the company or to another company.

By siphoning funds from reliability testing and quality control to ensure that production targets are met, the project chief is behaving rationally. It is a logical response to the apparently rigid use of the AIS. Extending the dimensions on which performance is measured and de-emphasising the short term may help to overcome this behaviour.

Reference : Ritti, R.R. and G.R. Funkhouser (1977), <u>The Ropes to Skip and the Ropes to Know</u>, Grid.

2.   The main features of the AIS recognized in the text are the need for participation, the relationship between financial performance measures and incentive schemes and the style of evaluation. The appropriateness of combinations of these features depends on the orientation of the management control system and the way the individual company has responded to environmental uncertainty and diversity.

(a) The actual production process for standard steel rods may be viewed as tending towards a programmed activity. If production is characterized by repetitive actions, a known and predictable relationship between inputs and outputs, then the need for participation by the production manager is lessened. A reward scheme strictly linked to physical or financial measures of output may be appropriate to encourage the manager to meet predetermined targets. Evaluation on a short-term basis appears relevant.

(b) The production of microchips may also be viewed as a programmed decision-making activity. However, when the microchips are capable of being customized to client specifications and technological advances and end product uses are continually changing, the need to be responsive may suggest elements of non-programmed decision-making. The divisional manager may be best placed to re-act or pro-act to these changes and his may be the best predictive model. Hence, his active

170

participation in planning will be required. A strict relationship between the short-term financial performance of his division and his own promotion prospects or cash bonus may encourage this participation to be less than honest. Therefore, longer-term evaluation encompassing qualitative and non-financial quantitative measures of performance may be called for.

(c) The strengths of the company which have created the brand leader image must be uncovered. Production efficiency may suggest that an AIS having similar design features to the steel rods example is merited. If marketing effectiveness is an important element in the company's success, an AIS similar to that suggested in the microchip example seems appropriate. Therefore, within a particular company it may be necessary to design an AIS which is flexible and reflects the different degrees of non-programmed decision-making undertaken by different managers.

(d) The appropriate AIS depends on the stability of the relationships between the gas producing division and the user divisions. A corporate policy which inhibits the gas producing division from seeking external customers means that it effectively services internal demand only. Production plans are therefore dependent on the other divisions and if their demands are predictable and do not significantly change, then an AIS suitable for programmed decision-making appears appropriate. Little or no participation in planning is required and a short-term evaluation on financial performance measures linked to rewards is likely to motivate the gas producing divisional manager to provide an efficient service.

Reference : Gordon, L.A. and D. Miller (1976)

3. (a)

	Standard Cost	Actual	Variance
Production	8.8 million	8.8 million	
DL worked	22 000 hours	18 000 hours	
Materials used	110 000 lbs	104 000 lbs	

Costs

DL	22 000	21 600	400 F
DM	55 000	62 400	7400 A
Overhead costs – Fixed	44 000	49 000	5000 A
– Variable	66 000	64 000	2000 F
Total costs	187 000	197 000	10 000 A
Revenue	264 000	264 000	-
Net Profit	77 000	67 000	10 000 A

Overhead computation:

Single overhead: $\dfrac{100\,000}{20\,000}$ = £5 per d.1.hr Fixed 40 20 = £2p d.1hr

Var. 60 20 = £3p d.1hr

Flexed budget overhead = £110 000

Fixed 22 000 x 2 = 44 000

Variable 22 000 x 3 = 66 000

172

Analysis of Variance

Direct labour

Rate AH (AR–SR)	18 000(1.2 – 1)	=	3600 A
Efficiency SR (AH–SH)	1 (18 000 – 22 000)	=	<u>4000</u> F
			<u>400</u> F

Direct material

Price AQ(AP–SP)	104 000 (0.6 – 0.5)	=	10 400 A
Usage SP(AQ–SQ)	0.5(104 000 – 110 000)	=	<u>3 000</u> F
			<u>7 400</u> A

4 Way Analysis of Overheads

Budget	Actual – Flexed at act. hours		
	113 000 – (40 000 + 3 x 18 000)	=	19 000 A
Capacity	Flexed – Overhead applied at act. hours		
	94 000 – (5 x 18 000)	=	4000 A
Efficiency	Var.O'h'd Rec'y Rate (A.H. – S.H.)		
	3 (18 000 – 22 000)	=	12 000 F
Effectiveness	Total O'h'd Rec'y Rate (AH – SH) – Efficiency		
	5 (18 000 – 22 000) – (+12 000)	=	<u>8000</u> F
			<u>3000</u> A

3 Way Analysis of Overheads

Fixed Overhead:	Spending	(49000 – 40000)	9000 A
	Denominator	(40000 – 44000)	4000 F
Variable Overhead:	Spending	(64000 – 54000)	10000 A
	Efficiency	(54000 – 66000)	12000 F
			3000 A

Profit Reconciliation

Volume variance	(Original budget - Flexed)	7000 F
Operating variance	(Flexed budget - Actual)	10000 A
Actual - Budgeted Profit		£ 3000 A

The budget variance on overhead should be investigated fully. It is a spending variance and the only overhead variance potentially under the control of the manager. The overhead efficiency variance confirms the favourable direct labour usage. The capacity and effectiveness variances are merely due to flexing the fixed overhead budget.

The material price variance is also sufficiently large to merit investigation. The cause of the variance may be due to entirely external circumstances or a change in purchasing policy, lack of future contracts at fixed prices or manufacturing supervisors requesting higher quality material. The latter may help to explain the favourable material usage and direct labour efficiency variances.

(b) The need for participation may be argued to vary with the degree of non-programmed decision-making. From the little information available, it appears that the department's work is generally repetitive, capable of being planned in detail and is not subject to great complexity. There is a stable product range, a single technology and the size of the department may not merit decentralization.

The benefits to be derived from allowing participation by the supervisors is therefore limited. In fact, it seems that the supervisors have mis-used their discretion by providing 'loose' standards for the workers to aim for. Brian's first step should be to meet with the supervisors to discover how the assumptions on which the standards were revised compared with actual events.

(c) Lowe and Shaw (1968) suggest that managers bias budgets:

> (i)   in response to implied corporate policies viz., sales growth is x% p.a.
>
> (ii)   in order to over-attain expected performance and thereby improve their rewards
>
> (iii)   in response to previous poor performance in order to regain superior approval at least in the short-run.

Hence, bias can be upward or downward, intentional or unintentional (Schiff and Lewin, 1970) and is very difficult to identify. Counter-bias may demotivate an honest participant and/or create unrealistic budget targets. Ijiri, Kinard and Putney suggest :

$$k_1 (A) - k_2 |A - B|$$

as a means of eliminating bias but the weightings of k_1 and k_2 are unfortunately arbitrarily determined.

(d) If the programmed characteristics of the rubber hose activity are recognized, participation appears unnecessary. The supervisors may perceive that their performance is measured by means of an analysis of variances and this may be sufficient reason to put forward biased forecasts. A reward scheme associated with the analysis will encourage bias. Hence, Brian should reappraise the need for participation.

Reference : Yetton, P.W. (1976)

Further Reading : Milani, K. (1975) 'The Relationship of Participation in Budget-Setting to Industrial Supervisor Performance and Attitudes: A Field Study', The Accounting Review, April, pp. 274-284.

4   (a)

Total annual capacity = $\dfrac{252\,000 \times 100}{70}$ =   360 000

Total available capacity per month	30 000
Present utilization	21 000
Available	9000

Supplying the chain store order is feasible

Expected utilization $\dfrac{25\,000}{30\,000}$ =   83%+

Incremental Analysis for Typical Month

Revenue (4000 x 1.75)		£7000
Material (4000 x 0.65)		2600
Wages (1000 x 0.80)	800	
3000 x 1)	3000	3800
Sundry Plant expense		
(4000 x 0.24)		960
		7360

Less contribution to sister division

$0.6(2600) - 0.6(0.6(2600))$		624
		6736
Incremental contribution per month		£ 264

Assumptions : All costs included are realistic replacement costs now and will hold for the year. Depreciation is calculated over time and not use. Chain store sales will not affect existing sales.

(b) Material not transferred in: H.C.   1040

NRV	1500	
- 10%	150	1350
Conversion: R.C.	3100	
	-1100	2100 net savings

Material costs now become

Opp.cost (40%)		2100
Transferred in (60%)	1560	
Less cont.	624	936
		£3036

As compared with $2600 - 624 =$ 1976

The chain store order produces

an incremental loss   =   £ 796

Therefore do not accept order.

(c) Two important points arise. The decision to accept or reject is being taken from the company's perspective.

The divisional manager in (a) making Twisteze would not accept the order because the transfer price creates a divisional loss of $624 - 264 = £360$.

177

Secondly, the opportunity cost information is generally not imputed to control statements. Hence, if the transfer pricing problem could be overcome, the divisional manager may erroneously accept the order because it improves his short-term performance by £264.

(d) The four necessary conditions for effective control are:

    (i)   clear objective(s)

    (ii)   accurate measurement of actual performance

    (iii)   the provision of a predictive model

    (iv)   the availability of alternative actions.

In terms of (ii) and (iii), different accounting information is used for planning (incremental, opportunity cost) and control (full cost, historical cost, allocations). Managers may take decisions using the 'wrong' information given an emphasis on short-term control reports within the particular company. Behaviour congruence is unlikely to be attained by the traditional AIS when there is a high incidence of non-programmed decision-making.

5. (a)

	Material quantity purchased	5200 lbs
	Unfavourable unit price (£2.00 – £2.10)	£ 0.10
(i)	Unfavourable purchase price variance	£520.00 A
	Material quantity used	5300 lbs
	Material quantity required at standard for 5000	
	units produced (5000 unit times 1lb/unit)	5000 lbs
	Unfavourable quantity	300 lbs
	Standard price per pound	£ 2.00
(ii)	Unfavourable materials efficiency variance	£600.00 A

	Direct labour used	8200	hours
	Unfavourable unit hourly rate (£4.00-£4.10)	£0.10	
(iii)	Unfavourable direct labour price variance	£820.00 A	
	Direct labour used	8200	hours
	Direct labour required at standard for		
	5000 units produced	8000	hours
	Unfavourable direct labour used	200	hours
	Standard wage rate per direct labour hour	£4.00	
(iv)	Unfavourable direct labour efficiency variance	£800.00 A	

The overhead included in the standard unit costs is not explicitly related to direct labour cost. Thus, it seems appropriate to develop the over-head budget on the basis of output. The budget formula is £7250 per month (£87 000 – 12) plus £3.00 per unit (£180 000 ÷ 60 000 units).

	Actual Overhead Charged	Overhead Budget (for 1 month Period and 5000 unit output)	Variance (under) over budget
Indirect labour	£ 9840	£10000	(£160)
Supplies -- oil	3300	2500	800
Other variable overhead	3200	2500	700
Total variable overhead	£16340	£15000	£1340
Supervision	2475	2250	225
Depreciation	3750	3750	-0-
Other	1250	1250	-0-
Total fixed overhead	7475	7250	225
Total overhead	£23815	£22250	
Overhead budget variance			£1565

b) Clearly indicating where the responsibilities for price and quantity variance lie and charging the variance to the departments with initial responsibility reduces the conflict but does not eliminate it.

The specific cause(s) of the variance needs to be determined before there can be certainty that the proper department is charged. For example, if materials were purchased at higher than standard prices because the manufacturing department required a rush order, then the price variance is the ultimate responsibility of the manufacturing department. If the materials provided by the purchasing department were of slightly lower quality specifications than required, due to careless purchasing, the excess quantity used by manufacturing is the responsibility of the purchasing department.

180

Even if the variances are properly charged to the two departments, it can be argued that the purchasing department's variance is influenced by the excess quantity required by manufacturing. In this problem the extra 300 pounds will increase the purchasing department's variance (accumulated over several periods) by £30.00 (300 lbs times £0.10). The £30.00 is the joint responsibility of the two departments.

(c) The manufacturing department manager cannot control the price of the overhead items. Therefore the prices should not influence the data in his report. Further, the allocation method for service department costs is not sufficiently explained to identify what part if any of the variation can be identified with the department. The fixed overhead items listed in this problem normally are outside the control of a department manager. Supplies and indirect labour are left.

Control can be exercised at the departmental level over the amount of things used; therefore, emphasis should be placed on the quantities within the variances with little or no emphasis on the financial values. The major use of the financial values would be to establish the quantity level of each variance that would be economically worth management attention.

181

To: Department Management - Manufacturing

From :   Performance Analysis

Subject: Controllable Overhead

         Performance – November

	Controllable Overhead Items	Quantity	Percentage Compared to standard
A.	Indirect labour		
	Favourable indirect labour use		
	(value £400)	100 hours	4%
B.	Unfavourable oil use		
	(value £500)	1,000 gallons	20%

Commentary:

The value of the oil variation and its large percentage require that the cause be identified and control procedures applied. The indirect labour variation, although favourable, should be investigated to be sure that it does not represent unaccomplished activities that affect other aspects of the operations.

Calculation for Memorandum

Supplies – oil	6000 gallons
oil consumed	
Standard quantity for 5000	
units output	<u>5000</u> gallons
Unfavourable oil consumption	<u>1000</u> gallons
Value at standard oil prices	<u>£500</u> A

Indirect labour	
Hours used	2400
Hours standard for 5000	
units output	
(5000 times 0.5 hours)	2500
Favourable indirect labour	
variation	<u>100</u> hours
Value at standard wage rates	<u>£400</u> F

(d) The immediate reaction might be to dismiss the department manager. However, careful thought would require analysis of the situation to determine (i) if, on an overall basis, the department is being operated economically (if so, then dismissal may be undesirable); and (ii) if the cause of such behaviour is due to management reaction to unfavourable variances without regard to size or to undue emphasis by management on individual variances to the exclusion of measurement of overall performance.

If it is assumed that the manager is performing satisfactorily on an overall basis and should not be dismissed, then two possible solutions can be considered:

(i)   Revise reporting methods so as to emphasize overall performance.

(ii) Revise reporting on labour to combine direct and indirect labour into a single item for performance evaluation.

The crucial consideration is how to measure whether the manager is performing satisfactorily on an overall basis. This may require qualitative and quantitative non-financial performance measures to be developed.

6.   (a) The unusual features are the inclusion of key assumptions for expected and actual, the break-down of costs by controllable and non-controllable and the expression of service costs in non-financial terms. An analysis of performance may be based equally on deviations from the expected assumptions as on the budget.

(b) Explanations of what caused the reduced profit will not be confined to accounting data alone. Was the change in sales due to the introduction of the competitor's product? Did the union's disagreement account for the change in labour costs and productivity? An appraisal of the key assumptions themselves as well as their impact on the financial performance of the division can be undertaken.

(c) This form of report may be most appropriate in the multidivisional company where there is a high incidence of non-programmed decision-making. At least an equal emphasis should be placed on the divisional manager's ability to develop a feasible predictive model, to identify key variables and to be aware of how these effect financial performance. Feed forward controls may be improved by top management supplying assumptions about the general economic climate which form the parameters for the divisional manager's specific assumptions concerning garden tools and utensils. The comparison of assumptions therefore allows both levels of management to learn more about the changing environment.

(d) Identifying key assumptions at the planning or budget setting stage and comparing their effect on actual financial performance in a democratic, existential atmosphere should allow learning to take place. Recognition of changes in key assumptions should be reported upon immediately and informally. The accountant would seem to have a useful monitoring role to play in discerning these changes and also in helping the divisional management to interpret the financial effects of the changes. Hence frequent, informal contact may characterize the future relationship of the accounting staff and divisional management.

Further reading :   Lowe, E.A. and J.L.J. Machin (1983)

CHAPTER 14

MANAGEMENT CONTROL CASE STUDIES

PERMACLEAN PRODUCTS PLC

DESCRIPTION

The central issue in the Permaclean case is basically one of product pricing, but the analysis requires the estimation of appropriate costs from the accounting data which is provided, and also the construction of a rudimentary price-demand curve from information about past sales. It also permits the use of linear regression analysis in forecasting expected industry demand, although this is not essential.

The case provides a relatively simple situation for the student to analyse, but one which captures the major elements of a real-life pricing problem. However, there is sufficient information in the case for it to provide the basis for a full decision analysis, using either a decision tree approach or a simulation model.

USE OF THE CASE

I have found this case helpful in two situations. It provide a useful summary case for students completing a basic management accounting course where the topics of variable costing and pricing have been addressed. Such students may require to be given some guidance as to the approach expected of them. Alternatively, I have used it as the first case in a more advanced management control systems course at both undergraduate and Masters level. The accounting information provided is sufficiently confusing to require students to have to think quite carefully about how they are to proceed. It therefore serves to sharpen up previously acquired skills. Finally, the case is sufficiently open-ended to allow it to lead into a more extended discussion of several topics, such as :

186

(a) Problems in interpreting standard management accounting data, produced on both full and variable costing principles, and the provision of relevant data for management decision-making.

(b) Issues in pricing, including the advantages that can be obtained from differential pricing.

(c) The use of more advanced analytic techniques, such as decision tree analysis or simulation.

TEACHING NOTE

At its simplest, the problem facing the company can be reduced to making a choice between two alternative strategies. Either it can maintain its present, high price, policy and suffer a continuing fall in demand, or it can revert to its previous policy of seeking a competitive price. This latter policy can best be interpreted as pricing at the top end of the competitors' price range. A further alternative that might be considered is for predatory pricing below the competition, but this raises more complicated marketing issues. An analysis of these alternatives requires the following steps:

(a) Projection of total industry demand for 1988.

(b) Estimation of Permashine's market share, at various possible prices.

(c) Estimation of the variable costs of production.

(d) A contribution analysis using this information.

Total industry sales are best represented on a graph, from which a steadily rising trend can be discerned, despite a slight drop in 1984. If a straight line is fitted to all seven year data by linear regression it is found that

$$\text{Sales ('000s)} = 1171 + 141 \times (\text{Year number} = 1 \text{ to } 7)$$

187

giving a prediction of 2900 for 1988. However, this is exactly equal to 1987 sales, and recent history indicates a more rapidly rising trend. The final four years of data give a regression line of:

Sales ('000s) = 1165 + 245 x (Year number = 4 to 7)

and a prediction for 1988 of 3125. It would appear that Mr Williams' estimate of 3 000 000 bottles for 1988 is probably conservative, although a slight drop was experienced in one previous year. A range from 2 850 to 3 200 would cover the reasonably possible outcomes.

The market share for Permashine will obviously depend upon the price charged. The only information for which we have reliable data is for the 99p price, and for a price set at the top end of the competitors' range (1981–1985) which is equivalent to a price of 80p in 1987. (Perhaps we ought to consider inflationary trends into 1988, but these are likely to be quite small, and the analysis may be best conducted in terms of 1987 price levels and then adjusted to 1988 levels.)

At the higher price, market share fell by 5.5% in the first year and a further 4% in the second year, indicating a considerable degree of product loyalty. This fall also seems consistent with Mr Williams' view that there is a floor below which demand will not fall, although it is not clear on what evidence he bases his opinion. It is therefore reasonable to predict that market share may well fall by a further 3.5% in 1988 if the 99p price is maintained, giving a demand of (3 000 x 10% =) 300 000 bottles in 1988. A range of 250 000– 350 000 bottles would cover most of the likely possibilities.

If the price is dropped to the top end of the competitors' range (i.e. 80p) we could probably assume that the previous market share of 24% could be attained again. The real question is how long it will take to achieve this level of sales. The market was sticky in a downward direction; how sticky will it be upwards? This is difficult to answer, but my own inclination is to think that it may take a couple of years to regain the previous position; some of those who gave up Permaclean because of its price may be satisfied with a competing product and not return. Thus the movement from 13.5% share back to 24% may well yield only 18% or 19% share in 1988. Such a view is also consistent with Mr Williams' assertion that a price of 75p would give a 20% market share in 1988. Thus, the best prediction of demand in 1988 is probably 540 000 bottles at a price of 80p (and maybe 600 000 bottles at 75p).

Finally, there is the issue of estimating the variable costs of production. The direct labour and materials costs are clearly variable, with perhaps a slight increase in labour costs (due to overtime?) at the higher end. Departmental overhead also seems to be categorised correctly, with the fixed element being equivalent to an annual cost of £36 000. (There is a misprint on the fixed cost at 400 000 bottles, which should read 9p rather than 8p.) Factory overhead is more difficult to assign; however it can only refer to items not attributable to the Department (as these would come under Departmental overhead). Although it appears to be a variable cost, this is only because it is allocated on the basis of direct labour costs. It is possible that it contains a small variable element (e.g. electricity costs, if these are not separately metered) but it must also include substantial fixed elements (e.g. rates). However, it is small in total and no great damage will be done to the analysis if it is assumed to be totally fixed. Selling and administration costs are almost certainly totally fixed, for the sales force is remunerated on the basis of a salary, not commission. Thus the truly variable costs amount to about 35p per bottle (i.e. 17.5p + 8p + 9p + a small proportion of 3.5p).

We are now in a position to perform a contribution analysis. At the 99p price :-

Contribution   =   300 000 x (99p – 35p)   =   £192 000

At the 80p price :

Contribution   =   540 000 x (80p – 35p)   =   £243 000

At the 75p price :

Contribution   =   600 000 x (75p – 35p)   =   £240 000

Thus the lower prices are clearly better than the highest, although there is little to choose between 80p and 75p. Such a choice would require more information.

A decision tree analysis with most likely, optimistic and pessimistic industry sales forecasts and market shares could also be performed, again using two or three possible prices. Crudely, even if pessimistic forecasts are made for the performance with an 80p price, and compared with optimistic forecasts at the 99p price, the ordering of the alternatives is only just reversed :

Contribution (opt)   =   375 000 x (99p – 35p)   =   £240 000

Contribution (pess)   =   500 000 x (80p – 35p)   =   £225 000

Overall, there is every likelihood that the lower price will give the better results. However, even with the lower price it is probable that not more than 600 000 bottles will be sold, compared with a plant capacity of 800 000, and a marginal cost of production of about 35p. It may therefore be possible for Permaclean to find another outlet for this unused capacity. For example it may wish to consider export sales, bulk sales to commercial cleaning firms, or the production of a supermarket own label product. Provided these additional sales do not affect existing sales of Permaclean, any price in excess of the marginal cost of production (plus any additional costs incurred in meeting the special order) will generate additional contribution to profit.

190

To extend the discussion along these lines, students can be asked to give examples of products which are commonly sold at different prices. Supermarket 'own' brands, electricity and telephone services, British Rail fares and airlines provide some examples. In general, if a market can be effectively segmented, differential pricing provides improved contribution because those consumers willing to pay more than the lower 'market' price are made to do so, whilst only those who would not buy at the higher price are given the benefit of the lower price. The art lies in segmenting the market!

SCOVILL, INC.: NUTONE HOUSING GROUP

Teaching Note

The Scovill Inc.: NuTone Housing Group case describes a conflict between a corporate controller and a group vice president about cost accounting standards. The group vice president had his cost accounting system designed with standards that intentionally overstated product costs to affect pricing decisions and protect margins. The controller objected because the biased standards caused monthly and quarterly profits to be understated, because they allow the group to manipulate its earning figures, and because he was worried that management did not know its real product costs.

The case is designed to serve two main purposes. One is to motivate a philosophical discussion of cost accounting systems. In particular, should cost accounting systems be designed to provide costs as accurately as possible? Or should they be designed with biases in them if, as in this case, management feels those biases improve decision making?

The other purpose is to provide an opportunity to discuss the role of the corporate controller in a decentralized organization. The specific issue in this case is: Where do the authorities and responsibilities for the accounting system lie in a decentralized organization? This issue is complicated in this case because the controller is new to the company.

A 22-minute videotape, entitled Scovill Inc.: NuTone Housing Group (5-187-054) is available for use in this case. It shows Bob Hager, Scovill's new treasurer/controller, and Bill Hanks, manager of cost accounting and payroll at NuTone, answering questions in an MBA classroom in the spring of 1986. The tape shows that the disagreements persisted for years after the case, and it reveals the company's "solution" to the issue.

This teaching note was written by Associate Professor Kenneth A. Merchant as an aid to instructors in the classroom use of the Scovill, Inc.: NuTone Housing Group case (9-186-136).

Suggested Assignment Questions

1. Account for the following events as would be done in the
    NuTone division of Scovill:

    In a past year, the NuTone division of Scovill built
    1,000 units of one model of paddle fans. The standard
    and actual direct material was $20 per unit. The
    standard cost for a direct labor hour was $8.00. The
    total actual direct labor hours used were 400, and the
    workers were paid an average hourly rate of $10
    (including incentives) because the average direct labor
    efficiency rate was 300% (so the standard direct labor
    hours were 1,200). The overhead rate in the plant was
    150%. Over the course of the year, 500 of the units were
    sold at a price of $60 each. At year-end, a physical
    inventory was taken. The count revealed 400 good units
    left in inventory, and they were valued at an average
    cost of $30 each.

2. What, if anything, should Bob Hager do about the
    accounting system used in the NuTone division?

        The first question which, alternatively, can be posed and
solved during class, helps make sure the students understand the accounting
methods described in the case. The second question poses the key action
issue in the case.

Discussion of Question 1

        The solution to the first question in T-account format is as
follows:

Inventory				Cash or (Payables)				Overhead Applied	
) 20	(4) 22			(5) 30	(1) 20				(3) 6
) 4					(2) 4				
) 6									
) 4									
d 12				end 6					

Sales			CGS (standard)		
	(5) 30		(4) 22	(6) 4	

Description of Journal Entries:

(1) Material charged to inventory ($20 x 1000). This is not issue in
     this case.
(2) Actual direct labor costs charged to inventory (400 hr. x $10).
(3) Overhead applied to inventory at 150% of direct labor.

(4) Inventory to CGS. Standard cost = M + L + OH = 20 + [(1200 x $8.00) ÷ 1,000 units] + $9.60 x 1.5 = $44/unit. $44 x 500 units = $22,000.

(5) Sales for cash.

(6) Conversion cost adjustment. To have ending inventory equal $12,000 (400 x $30), inventory must be debited by $4,000. The offsetting credit goes to CGS. This $4,000 is the net amount of the favorable labor overhead variances less the unfavorable effects of scrap, shrinkage, etc.

Discussion of Question 2

The second question should generate some controversy. Bob Hager has three main alternatives:

1. Do nothing, or at least wait a while.

2. Fix the earnings problem by estimating the effect on profit monthly and writing journal entries to build up negative reserves that will offset the positive variance NuTone will turn in at year-end.

3. Get the system fixed. As persuading Jim Rankin (NuTone president) seems to have failed, Bob's main alternative is to take the issue to the audit committee of the board of directors in hope that it will force Mr. Rankin to make the change. Bob does not have the power to make the change unilaterally.

The arguments for and against making NuTone "fix" its cost accounting system are discussed in the case, but it is useful to summarize them on the blackboard and discuss their merit because judgments as to the worthiness of them lead directly to the solution.

The arguments in favor of fixing the problem are:

1. Can NuTone management know what its 5,000 products really cost without an accurate cost system? If not, decisions about pricing, product offerings, etc. are likely being made incorrectly.

2. The division is at considerable risk if Jim Rankin, who apparently has the best knowledge of product costs, leaves the company or is incapacitated.

3. Monthly and quarterly earnings for the division are distorted, and the distortion is getting larger. If the NuTone division is having operating problems, management may not see them in a timely manner because the trends in the financial statements are misleading. Furthermore, Scovill is a publicly held company, and investors and potential investors may be misled.

4. NuTone is using the cushion it builds up in its understated inventory to manage earnings from month to month. Fixing the system would quash this spirit of gamesmanship (or perhaps drive it elsewhere).

5. The large favorable variances at year-end easily cover a set of unfavorable variances (e.g., scrap, shrinkage) and may reduce management's incentive to develop effective systems and procedures to reduce them.

From Hager's viewpoint, the arguments in favor of <u>not</u> fixing the system are:

1. NuTone has been successful for a long time. Scovill is a highly decentralized organization--leave the division alone, unless major problems are indicated. This is an area for division-management discretion.

2. The earnings-distortion problem can be fixed with a few simple journal entries.

3. Bob Hager is new on the job. He should not cause a conflict with a senior line manager, at least not so early in his tenure.

4. The cost of switching could be major. It could involve developing standards for 50,000 labor operations.

5. The change would force changes in the division's way of doing business. Management is used to the information it receives, and the factory employees are used to their unique incentive system. Fixing the system may destroy many of the good ways of operating the division has developed over the years.

Rankin may have some other reasons for not wanting to change:

1. He likes being a "hero" at year-end when he turns in a large profit number, causing the corporation to meet its targets.

2. He is afraid of the negative variances and greatly values conservative accounting.

3. He virtually always meets his monthly budget targets because he has hidden profits he can call on as needed.

4. He maintains centralized control over the business because he is the only person who understands the real costs.

Pedagogy

It is important that the students understand the mechanics of NuTone's system before the qualitative issues are discussed. Therefore, with an inexperienced class, it is useful to start by going through the numerical example, whether or not it has been assigned for homework.

After that, the class lends itself nicely to an unstructured discussion. One approach is to clarify Bob Hager's alternatives and ask students what he should do. The arguments for and against each alternative and discussions as to their merits come out easily.

195

Another approach is to ask students if this issue is something that warrants a great deal of concern. You can ask if this is a "tempest in a teapot" or if "Hager has been an accountant too long." This approach motivates a broader discussion of the purpose of cost accounting standards, but it leads to the same end result. This way of conducting the discussion places a greater burden on the instructor to organize the comments made.

Students tend to make some speculations about the situation that are incorrect. These speculations are debunked in the videotape. If they arise before the videotape is shown, it is best to close them off immediately.

- Bob Hager was not brought in to fix this problem. It was a surprise to him when he arrived.

- At the time of the case, Bob had discussed the NuTone cost accounting issue with Len Leganza (executive vice president, finance) and Bill Andrews (president), but he had not been able to convince either that the issue was worth worrying about.

- The rise in inventories at NuTone over the period 1978-81 was not caused by poor inventory control. It is due to the shift toward sourcing from the Far East. Many NuTone inventories were in transit.

Some students also conclude that Nutone management can augment their incentive compensation through this biased cost accounting system. This is not true. The system only moves income between months and quarters. The biases (and income) are straightened out at year end.

After about 40 minutes (in an 80-minute class), I have the students vote as to what they would do if they were Bob Hager. About half of the students want to fix the problem now. The others are split about equally between doing nothing and writing journal entries to solve the earnings problem only.

Then I show the videotape which reveals what happened in the company. At the start of the tape, announce that the first speaker is Bob Hager (controller) and that the other is Bill Hanks (Nutone's cost accounting manager). The tape reveals that at the end of 1982, the favorable variance grew to $7 million, and the audit committee ordered Bob Hager to get the problem fixed. NuTone responded with a system that calculated what they called "actual standards" from the last ten times a particular operation was worked on. Use of these new standards caused the factorable variances to go down significantly. In 1985, the corresponding number was $396,000. However, the NuTone division continued its old cost accounting system and used the biased product costs for making decisions.

196

BBR plc

DESCRIPTION

This case highlights the classical transfer pricing problem where divisions operating in their own interests may reduce total company profitability. In addition to the computations using marginal analysis, the potential costs and benefits of a transfer pricing procedure based on divisional management negotiation are investigated. The trade off between head office involvement as mediator or arbitrator which may allow optimal economic decisions and a 'hands-off' policy which promotes decentralised profit responsibility but with the danger of sub-optimal decision-making can be explored.

USE OF THE CASE

When exploring the many transfer prices which are used in practice and advocated in theory, it is relatively easy to underplay the importance of the procedures whereby the transfer price is set. This case is useful in recognizing the fact that the ultimate transfer price is only a part of a transfer pricing system which includes administrative procedures. The procedures, as much as the transfer price itself, can influence the degree of control and responsibility which divisional managers perceive they exercise.

At the postgraduate or final year undergraduate level, the case allows re-inforcement of economic marginal analysis and its defects, places the transfer pricing system in an organizational context and has provided a springboard for a far-reaching discussion about implications of alternative transfer pricing systems.

It is feasible with a well prepared class to cover these issues within a one hour period. The open-ended discussion of alternatives and their implications may lead to greater time being taken.

EXPLANATION OF GIDDINGS' ARGUMENT

Preston Division

Output	Total Cost (£000's)	Marginal Cost (£000's)	TotalRevenue at TP=£12.50	Marginal Revenue
100 000	1 300	-	1 250	-
2	2 500	1 200	2 500	1 250
3	3 660	1 160	3 750	1 250
4	4 680	1 020	5 000	1 250
5	5 550	870	6 250	1 250
6	6 300	750	7 500	1 250
7	6 860	560	8 750	1 250
8	7 280	420	10 000	1 250
9	7 560	280	11 250	1 250
1 000 000	7 700	140	12 500	1 250

Shrewsbury Division

Buy in Quantities	Total Cost	Marginal Cost
100 000	1 400	-
2	2 700	1 300
3	3 900	1 200
4	4 950	1 050
500,000	5 950	1 000

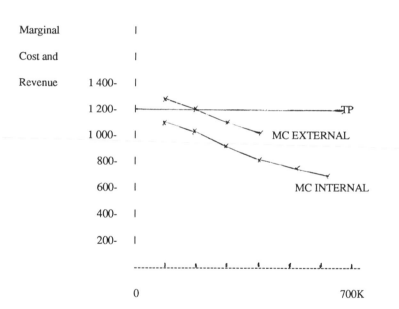

Marginal

Cost and

Revenue 1 400-

1 200- ⊢ ————————————————————TP

1 000- MC EXTERNAL

800-

600- MC INTERNAL

400-

200-

0   700K

Quantities

A comparison of the marginal costs of internal as opposed to external purchase reveals that the Shrewsbury Division should buy internally. However, Giddings will base his decision on the price he is charged, the £12.50 transfer price and the external suppliers' price.

POTENTIAL ACTIONS

If Giddings acts rationally, he should be willing to purchase at least 300000 metres of rubber hose internally, (£3.75m versus £3.9m).

In order to operate at full capacity, consistent with the objective of increasing market share, Giddings may buy externally either two lots of 100000 metres as he thinks is likely or one lot of 200000 metres. The total cost to his division of operating at full capacity is then £6.55m (£3.75 internally + £2.8m externally) and £6.45m respectively. Internal purchase of the total 500000 metres will cost £6.25m. However, Giddings argues that whilst lower than the feasible alternatives, the cost of internal trade at this level is £300000 more than if he were able to place the entire order externally.

Company's View	Gidding's View
Buy 300000 metres internally	£3750000 vs £3.9m
Cost £3660000	buy internally
Buy 500000 metres	£6250000 internally
Cost £5550000	£5950000 externally
	£6550000 mix internal + external
	£6450000 mix internal + external

Given the unavailability of an external supplier who will provide 500 000 metres of rubber hose, Giddings is faced with limited, uneconomic external purchasing, operating at below capacity or paying what he believes to be an 'unfair', uncompetitive transfer price to attain full capacity.

From the information given in the case (para. 2), it would seem that Giddings in the past has opted to operate at below capacity or bought externally at uneconomic prices. This may be logical from his point of view because it prevents a promotion competitor, the Preston Divisional Manager, being shown in a better light by scoring relatively higher profits. The negotiation process may also have had an impact causing Giddings' dysfunctional behaviour.

THE CURRENT PROCEDURE AND HIDDEN COSTS

Negotiated transfer prices (TP) appear consistent with a decentralized management control system. Both parties have the opportunity to discover each other's views, perspectives and opinions and the resulting TP may be seen as an integrating mechanism.

However, for the negotiated TP to be equally acceptable, both parties must be able to provide verifiable data to the discussion. Shrewsbury is using list prices which may be based on past market conditions and the discounts may not have been subject to actual past transactions. Preston incorporates cost data from the central purchasing office without knowing whether these are relevant or accurate. Both parties may have legitimate differing views of the future market conditions and, coupled with the discount structure, the price range over which the negotiations could wander appears wide. At these volumes of inter-divisional trade, a price alteration of only pence per metre may result in significant changes in the profits reported for each division.

The danger is that the negotiations may become a feuding ground where animosity and retribution occur rather than cooperation, because of dissatisfaction with past TP 'agreements'. The best poker player may win. Divisional profit figures will not reflect economic efficiency nor managerial effectiveness. There is the real danger that parochial interest will become supreme and future collaboration, cross-fertilization between the divisions will not occur.

IMPROVEMENTS:

Having a Head Office (HO) mediator who excludes the most outlandish data and narrows the focus may improve the existing system. A HO arbitrator would take a more active role in the negotiations but there is no guarantee that he/she would not be drawn or be perceived as being drawn into the feuding.

A plausible alternative is to gain agreement on the TP by firstly agreeing the standard variable cost and then allocating a period cost (based on fixed and allocated costs) to represent the proportion of Preston's capacity earmarked for Shrewsbury. This ignores market conditions. Substituting an ex post contribution gained from external sales by Preston as the period cost may allow enhanced profit responsibility but this is so without its own difficulties (viz external purchasers' orders are in smaller volumes than internal orders).

BEECH PAPER COMPANY

DESCRIPTION

This is a role-playing version of the well-known Birch Paper Company case. The central issue is the negotiation of the price to be paid for a product being transferred between two of the company's operating divisions. However, it also raises much broader issues connected with organizational structure, performance measures and performance appraisal.

USE OF THE CASE

The case can be used with groups of two, three or four participants. The two central roles are those of Mr Clark and Mr Norton. Mr Hodge can be played by the teacher for several groups at a time, if necessary. Mr Sutherland's role is optional , but allows the negotiation to spread to a third division.

All participants are given the introductory information as far as the setting description (pp.412-414). Each Divisional Manager then receives his role description and budget data for his division alone. Mr Hodge is given copies of everything, possibly with several copies of the memo from his accountant, so that he can give it to divisional managers. Alternatively this memo can be omitted completely and the participants expected to derive it from the information given.

Although the case can be used to focus on issues of transfer pricing, I use it to bring out broader contextual and performance appraisal issues. The memo to Mr Hodge from his accountant serves to clarify the economic situation at an early stage. It can be omitted if students are required to develop its content independently, provided only to Mr Hodge or given to to all participants.

About one hour is required for students with good accounting knowledge to prepare their role, perhaps rather longer for Mr Hodge and less for Mr Sutherland. It is essential for Mr Clark and Mr Norton to be well prepared. Mr Hodge can skimp on preparation, but requires a greater maturity of judgement. Mr Sutherland's role is suitable for a less well briefed participant, as he will pick up a lot from the initial discussions which do not involve him directly.

I have found the case suitable for undergraduate and postgraduate accounting students, MBA students and also for practicing management accountants.

TEACHING NOTE

I usually introduce the case with a brief description of the context, and point out that there is one simplication from a real life situation; namely that the order is question represents a full year's supply of a product that would probably be the subject of a series of smaller negotiations throughout the year in practice. I also point out that the figures in all the draft budgets are intended to be consistent and are initially based on the assumption that the proposed transfer will go ahead at a price of £480 per thousand boxes. I then allow preparation time, followed by 30-60 minutes for the negotiations, with about 30-45 minutes for a final plenary session with all groups.

In the plenary session, I usually get each group to report on the final outcome. These generally include :-

(a) Internal transfer at about £410 per thousand

(b) Internal transfer between £440-450 per thousand

(c) External purchase from either Scott or Irish

(d) Imposition of a price by Mr Hodge

Before getting into an economic analysis, it can be useful to explore the feelings of the various participants as they started the negotiation process. Evidently the bottom-line budget figure has an enormous influence! The situation is difficult because there is no price at which both the Carton and Northern Divisions can break-even without the Southern Division changing its price.

It is then useful to clarify the economic situation. Crucial to this is the note at the bottom of the memo from Mr Hodge's accountant which indicates the analysis given there is valid only if slack capacity exists. It also requires other prices charged by the Carton Division to be unaffected. It may well be sensible of the Carton Division to plan to fill only 90% of its capacity with high margin business rather than fill it 100% at lower prices. If dropping the 20% markup internally would affect external pricing as Mr Clark claims, then it is better for the order to be placed externally.

Only when this preparatory work has been done can Mr Hodge's stance be sensibly discussed. If he intervenes he is necessarily making a judgement about the competence of one of his division managers, or at least likely to ultimately destroy the decentralized approach he has been building up. Sometimes the consequences of the 'hands off' decentralized approach need to be explored in some detail before students fully appreciate the benefits of this stance.

The main conclusions I try to draw from this use of the case are as follows :-

(a) The fundamental importance of the budgetary control structure in influencing managers' behaviour, especially when their performance is measure by reference to a budget figure.

(b) The close connection of accounting performance measures with the philosophy of management adopted by a company, its organizational structure, and the other control mechanisms it utilizes.

205

(c) The role of the specific performance measures used. The case is ambiguous about the role of the excess profit after the 6% deduction. Is this 'residual income' meant to be maximized, or is breakeven all that is required? Where did the 6% come from? Should it be the same for all divisions? How would behaviour have changed if it had been 4% or 8%?

(d) The issue is not one which can be sorted out by an accountant acting in isolation. It must involve the line managers, although the accountant can serve a vital role (e.g. note the usefulness of the memo to Mr Hodge).

(e) Communication and negotiation are important processes. In this role-playing situation it is very easy. How might things differ if the managers were at separate locations many mile apart? *(n.b. some groups could be structured so as to simulate this).*

ASSUMING CONTROL AT ALTEX AVIATION (A)

Teaching Note

I. Purpose of Case

   Two young and inexperienced MBAs purchase a small company that is
in financial trouble. It is not clear whether they can survive. If they
can, they believe it will only be done with tight cash management and new
accounting and control systems. They design a new system in which each
line of business is treated as a profit center and managed in a decentralized fashion. Operations during their first nine months are described and
documented. Follow-on cases [ALTEX AVIATION (A) (9-180-153) and (B) (9-180-154)]
describing and documenting the next eight years of the company's growth can
be used for another one or two days of class, if desired.

   ASSUMING CONTROL AT ALTEX (A) can be taught as a case in entrepre-
neurship or corporate strategy, but its primary purpose is as a stand-alone
case in the design of accounting and control systems for small companies.
In this setting it can communicate the following points:

1. The type of control system that will best serve an organization must
  be closely matched to the specific challenges (in this case illiquidity
  and negligible profitability), the nature of the company (in this case
  several very different lines of business), and the personality of the
  managers (in this case young and inexperienced).

2. Assuming that a decentralized control system is indicated, how do you
  design one? How do you handle

  a. transfer pricing,
  b. department manager autonomy,
  c. granting of credit and collection of receivables,
  d. purchasing and payment to suppliers, and
  e. allocation of administrative costs?

  The students have an opportunity to see that the design of each of
  these issues is, like the choice of system, dependent on the nature
  of the specific challenge, the business, and the personalities of
  the people.

This teaching note was written by Edmund M. Goodhue, Instructor, Assistant
Professor Kenneth A. Merchant, and Professor Neil C. Churchill as an aid to
instructors teaching ASSUMING CONTROL AT ALTEX AVIATION (A) (-183-058).

II. Teaching Strategy

Assignment Questions

        This case is so rich in detail that, unless the class is carefully
structured, discussion tends to focus on the "color" and quickly strays into
the entrepreneurial area. Thus, to achieve the teaching objectives, it is
better to ask specific questions of the students in advance to guide their
preparation and to keep the resulting class discussion focused on answering
those questions. One possible set of questions is

1.   Did Altex need a new control system at the time of the takeover?
2.   Evaluate the control system that Frank and Ted implemented. Should
     anything have been done differently?

        For entrepreneurship or strategy classes, this case can be followed
by ALTEX AVIATION (A) and (B) which tell what happened to the company over
the following eight years and discuss the issues of long-range planning and
making the transition from entrepreneurs to big company managers.

Time Management

        The following represents one possible set of questions the instruc-
tor can ask during class and the amount of time that might be allocated for
the resulting discussion.

Question	Time
A. Did Altex Need a New System?	
1. Did Altex meet their acquisition objectives?	5 minutes *
2. What are the most critical problems facing Altex at the takeover?	15
3. What does Ted see as the purpose of a control system?	10
4. Did Altex need a new system? (summary)	—
B. Evaluate the New System.	
1. What did Ted do?	30 **
2. Why no budgeting?	10
3. What kind of manager will Ted be?	5
4. What next?	—
C. Breaking the Disguise	5
TOTAL	80 minutes

        Each of these subtopics will now be covered in detail.

---

* Spend more time if taught as a strategy case.
**Spend less time if taught as a strategy case.

Did Altex meet their objectives?

Most students will agree that Altex met the criteria outlined on
page 2 of the case. Exhibit TN-1 shows the kind of chart that is useful to
elicit from the student discussion. It is relatively easy to fill in the
"pro" column. It is more instructive to get the students thinking about
the possible mistakes Frank and Ted made from the very beginning. The two
major mistakes were:

- They knew there was a high chance of failure (Page 3) and seemed to
  go ahead without any concern for the **implications** of failure. Specifically, they did not consider the effect on their credit ratings,
  career (delayed), or morale (shattered) if the company went under.
  Thus the "cost" of Altex was actually considerably **more** than $10,000.

- They seemed to ignore their 20% growth criterion. They did no studies
  to see if an FBO was a good business. In short, they made a classic
  manager's mistake of focusing on implementation detail prematurely--
  before fully determining the strategic validity of the project.

Unless this is taught as a strategy case, don't spend too much time on this
point. It is merely intended to get the class into the case.

What are the most critical problems for Altex?

On Page 7, Ted says that his key challenges are:

- cash,
- installing a control system to support management and provide
  information to make decisions, and
- taking control from Sarah.

The first question that must be answered by the student is, "How
is Altex doing now?" The first answer you are likely to get is "badly--
they lost $100,000 last year." A more careful analysis (Exhibit TN-2, Part
I) shows that Altex is currently losing "only" $20,000 on an annual basis.
This really doesn't address the issue of cash flow, however, and a very good
student will do the analysis of Part II of Exhibit TN-2. From this, a funds
flow can be estimated for the four months immediately preceding this acqui-
sition, Part III of Exhibit TN-2. This shows that ongoing cash needs are
approximately $20,000 every four months (to finance operating losses and
reductions in payables).

Frank and Ted's panic about cash seems unjustified. From Exhibit
TN-2 it appears that they have enough cash to last another year--even with
no improvement in operations. Cash control is critical, certainly, and is
a high priority, but perhaps not the all-consuming crisis implied by the
case.

The most important item is profitability. Ted seems to feel that
the primary way to achieve profitability is through better information.
Very few students will disagree. Some will argue, however, that a formal

control system is overkill in so small a company. With only $2 million in
sales, most entrepreneurs would collect information much less formally.
This raises one of the most interesting questions in the case: what is
Ted's view of the management process?

Ted's use of the control system

At the bottom of Page 7, Ted talks about using the control system
as the "black hat" in a process where managers have great freedom of action.
On the top of Page 8, Ted says that he doesn't have the time to exercise
more direct top-down decision-making. On these two pages and again on Page
17, Ted stresses his role as a teacher.

In defense of this style of management, students will make the
following points:

o   A formal system positions the company for growth.
o   It frees Ted's time to do more important things.
o   Decentralization gives authority and responsibility to department
     heads.

On the other hand, on the top of Page 3, Frank admits that one of
the reasons for decentralization is that he and Ted don't know the business.
From this (and for other reasons) some students will conclude that

o   Ted is using the control system to shore up his weaknesses--
     inexperience and lack of knowledge of the business.
o   It will all fail because you don't succeed by taking decisions
     away from people who don't know what they are doing (because of
     lack of industry knowledge) and give them to others who also
     don't know what they are doing (because of lack of management
     skills).
o   Decentralization is a sham--Frank and Ted will make all the
     decisions anyway.

A class discussion on this issue can become quite heated. After
five minutes or so, it is useful to ask, "how does Ted think the control
system is going to increase profitability?" The answer is not that managers
are going to be motivated because of information, decentralization, and the
joys of autonomy. Quite the opposite. On Page 7, Ted says that he wants
managers to make decisions "the way I would want them made." In other words,
Ted wants the control system itself to stand over a manager and tell him
what to do by providing "very fast feedback as to how they were doing and
[making] it personally worthwhile to them to do the right thing." The
resulting discussion should focus on whether this is possible or desirable.

What did Ted do?

This is the guts of the discussion if taught as a control case.
It can be divided into five subparts: cash, allocations, transfer pricing,
authority and responsibility, and information flow. The whole discussion
should take about 30 minutes.

1. Cash

It is interesting to start the discussion by asking, "Given their cash crisis, would you have given cash and credit to Will Leonard and Roy Douglas?" Most students will say "No way!" It is useful to encourage this attitude by pointing out that in reality it was a 20 year old surfer and a 5 year old retainer with no training who would now be in charge of cash.

Then you should ask, "What, exactly, did Ted give them?" A chart similar to Exhibit TN-3, Part I can be filled in.

You can then ask, "Why should receivables go down?" Some will say, "They won't." Others will point to the increasing charge for old receivables and the 10% commission as reasons why they should go down. Others will say that the dispatchers know the customers better and see them more often than Sarah Arthur did.

Then you can ask, "Did it work? Did receivables go down to generate more cash?" An analysis similar to Part II of Exhibit TN-3 can be done here. The answer is that the system cut receivables almost in half--from 33.5 days when they took over to 19 days 6 months later.

2. Allocations

You should then ask them about the allocation policy. The key thing to bring out is that the dollar amount allocated was known in advance by each manager or was a percent of something over which the manager had control. The purpose of this was to give managers a feeling of confidence in the "profit figures" on which their bonuses were based.

3. Transfer Pricing

If time is tight, skip this part. Otherwise, ask about the implications of the flight school going to a competitor for maintenance? What should Ted do if that happens once a week? Once a day? Even more interesting would be to spin the following tale.

One of Altex's competitors on the field offers the flight school a 40% discount on the labor rate if all maintenance is done at the competitor. The Altex shop manager replies that he isn't interested in matching the offer--his gross margin in 52.4% (case exhibit 8) and he doesn't want the hassle "for no profit." Assume that 30% of the shop's business comes from the flight school. The flight school manager tells Ted that he is using his authority to take the maintenance elsewhere. What should Ted do? For each possible action of Ted's, the cost to each department and to the company as a whole can be calculated and weighed against the impact on the motivation (and thus long-term profitability) of each manager by "violating" the "independence" policy.

4. Authority and Responsibility

The best way to introduce this topic is to ask what the class thinks of how Frank and Ted handled the beard issue. The class will be unanimously against their method. By now in the discussion, the value of the independence of department managers has been well established. After three or four minutes of unanimity it is useful to ask, "Well, what should Ted do if he truly feels that a department manager is making a bad decision about an esthetic issue? Or one of minor profit impact? Or major profit impact? Or aircraft safety? This is an interesting way to stretch the students' understanding of the real costs and benefits of autonomy.

5. Information Flow

A good way to start is to ask, "What do you think about the Daily Reports (Exhibit 9)?" It should be quite easy to have the students supply a table such as Exhibit TN-4. Almost everyone will agree on both the pros and cons. The decision should focus on what benefits you would give up to reduce the drawbacks.

Then you might ask, "What do you think of the Monthly Profit Center Reports (Appendix A)?" A table like Part II of Exhibit TN-4 can then be filled in by the students.

Finally, it is useful to ask the students about their reactions to Ted's approach to bankers. Should the bankers get the profit center reports (a 50-page package)? What are the risks of that strategy?

Why no budgeting?

You ask, "What kind of budgeting system does Ted have?" If there are blank stares, ask them to look at Appendix A where there is space specifically provided for budgets and variances, but no numbers appear.

Some students will be surprised that Ted, so (perhaps overly) complete in all other areas, seems to have "forgotten" to make a budget. Others will say, "But wait, who should make the budget in a decentralized environment --the department managers! So why didn't Ted show (force) them to make a budget?"

Then, if time permits, there can be a discussion about what it takes for a line manager, inexperienced at budgeting, to make his first budget. What tools would Ted have to provide (like historical figures for each month), and were those tools available?

It is particularly important to have this discussion if you are going to use ALTEX AVIATION (A) and (B) later on, for the issue of how to involve department managers in the planning process will surface eight years later as one of the central issues of ALTEX (B).

What kind of manager will Ted be?

The class will be divided on this issue. Some will feel that Ted
s a gutsy brilliant guy who is going to "make it happen." Others will feel
hat Ted is naive and covers his youth and inexperience with academic trivia
ike overly complex systems and blackboards in the office.

Those who support Ted will say, "Look, the proof is in the perfor-
ance!" and will cite Exhibits 1, 4 and 5 showing:

	Just Before (or at) Purchase	8 Months Later
Cash	$ 88,000	$129,000
Profitability	$(100,000) year	$240,000 annualized
Working Capital	$ 104,000	$327,000

This discussion is important in making students focus on the
ualities they think are important to success, including importantly the
roper role of control systems.

What next?

The purpose of this question is to get the students to summarize
heir feelings about the case and to provide a setting either to break the
isguise or lead in to ALTEX AVIATION (A).

II. Breaking the Disguise

Altex survived and grew over the following eight years to sales
f over $30 million and profits of over $1 million. The control system
emained in effect virtually unchanged and was credited by both Frank and
ed as being one of the key things that helped them achieve their growth.

The company was sold in the late 1970s for the equivalent of well
ver $3 million. Frank went on to become the chief financial officer of a
eal estate development firm, and Ted earned a second BS, went on to MIT
or graduate work, and is now at a well-known Eastern business school working
n his DBA and teaching control.

Frank is really Richard B. Fontaine (HBS '70) and Ted is really
ed Goodhue (HBS '70). Altex is Martin Aviation of Orange County, California.

ASSUMING CONTROL AT ALTEX AVIATION (A)

Exhibit TN-1

Did Altex Meet Their Acquisition Objectives?

Objective	Pro	Con
1. Cost nothing	Yes, only $10,000	o High chance of failure means career setback
		o Failure → confidence ruined
		o Failure → bad reputation and credit history
2. Need management skills	Yes, currently mismanaged	(none)
3. Fragmented and non-oligopolistic	o One of 8 companies on airport	(none)
	o Many similar companies in U.S.	
4. 20% annual growth	(none)	o They did no market surveys or other growth studies.

ASSUMING CONTROL AT ALTEX AVIATION (A)

Exhibit TN-2

How Healthy Is Altex?

I. Income Just Before Purchase (from Exhibit 2 in the case)

Department (fully allocated)	September-December 1981	
	4 Months	Annualized
Fuel	$ 26,176	$ 78,528
Service (Maintenance)	(13,462)	(40,386)
Parts	(2,425)	(7,275)
Flight School	(5,094)	(15,282)
Avionics	(1,020)	(3,060)
Aircraft Sales	(10,698)	(32,094)
	$ (6,523)	$(19,569)

Exhibit TN-2 (continued)

II. Balance Sheet ($000) (from Exhibit 1 of the case)

	8/26/71	Reclassify Contracts Receivable[2]	Convert Debt[3]	Sale and Leaseback Building[4]	Estimated Operations 9/71-12/71	1/1/72
Cash	$ 8			100	(20)	$ 88
Other Current Assets	288	(26)			27	289
Total Current Assets	$ 296					$ 377
Fixed Assets	484	26		(410)	(18)	82
Total Assets	$ 780					$ 459
Payables - Trade	174				(8)	166
Notes Payable	88		(50)		(7)	31
Other Current Liabilities	70				6	76
Total Current Liabilities	$ 332					$ 273
Long-Term Debt	465		50	(409)	18	124
Equity	(17)			99	(20)[1]	62
Total Liabilities and Equity	$ 780					$ 459

[1] From Exhibit TN-1

[2] From Footnote (c) of Exhibit 1

[3] Page 11 of the case

[4] There must have been a profit recorded on the sale of the building of $99,000--deduced from the need to reconcile equity. We also know that $100,000 was added to cash. We assume that $410 in assets and $409 in liabilities were removed from the balance sheet by the sale.

Exhibit TN-2 (continued)

II. <u>Estimated fund flow September-December 1971</u>

<u>Provided by</u>:

Increase in long-term debt	$ 18
Decrease in fixed assets	18
Increase in current liabilities	6
Decrease in cash	20
	$ 62

<u>Used for</u>:

Increase in current assets	27
Decrease payables	15
Operating loss	20
	$ 62

ASSUMING CONTROL AT ALTEX AVIATION (A)

Exhibit TN-3

Cash Control

I.

Department Responsible For	Accounting Responsible For

Department Responsible For
- o Granting credit
- o Collecting money
- o Maintaining A/R detail
- o Submitting balanced
     (error-free) daily
     reports

Accounting Responsible For
- o Maintaining A/R totals
- o Depositing money

II. Receivables ($000)

	Receivables ÷	Month's Sales[1]	= Collection Period (×30)
February	$52	$ 46.6[2]	33.5 days
May	73	119.1	18.4 days
August	91	139.7	19.5 days

[1] excluding aircraft sales

[2] $181 for January-February less $87.9 for aircraft = $93.1 ÷ 2
= $46.6 estimated for February

ASSUMING CONTROL AT ALTEX AVIATION (A)

Exhibit TN-3

I.   Daily Reports

            Pro   Con

o Catches errors at source   o Why should departments do
   (by forcing to balance   accounting? They should
   sales and receipts).   be doing marketing and
                                  production!

o Provides management daily
   sales, gross margin, and   o Too complex for an oper-
   cash figures.   ation with 10 people in
                                  it!

II.   Monthly Profit Center Reports

            Pro   Con

o Manager has information   o Can Will Leonard really
   to make decisions.   handle 8 pages of data
                                  each month? Much too
                                  much detail.

HCC INDUSTRIES, INC.

Teaching Note

Purpose of Case

The HCC Industries case was written to motivate a discussion of
the relationships between budget targets, performance evaluation procedures, and incentives in decentralized organizations. The situation
described in the case is dramatic because the company made a significant
shift in its philosophies about budgets and incentives.

Until 1987, HCC's operating units' budgets contained "stretch"
performance targets because corporate managers believed aggressive targets
would motivate the operating managers to perform at their highest possible
levels. In planning for fiscal year 1988, however, the corporate managers
changed the company's budgeting philosophy. They decided to have the units
work toward "minimum performance standard" (MPS) budget targets that were
"realistic" and achievable with 100% probability by an effective management
team. The corporate managers also changed the rewards attached to budget
achievement: If operating managers failed to achieve their MPS targets,
they earned no bonuses and were actually in danger of losing their jobs.

The case describes the company's management systems before and
after the change and the first-quarter experiences with the new systems.
The description at the end of the case suggests that the change was not
totally successful: None of the operating units achieved all of its MPS
targets, and organizational tension had increased significantly. This
outcome leaves students to ponder whether the failures lie in the new
budgeting philosophy or in the implementation of the change.

The teaching of the case can be supplemented by using a videotape
of HCC's president, Andy Goldfarb, discussing the company's experiences
with the new systems. The videotape is called HCC Industries: The Budgeting Philosophy, and What Happened (9-890-018). (The transcript of the tape
is 9-190-189.) Mr. Goldfarb's comments on tape suggest that he believes
that the first-quarter problems were primarily start-up problems.

Kenneth A. Merchant, Associate Professor, prepared this teaching note as an
aid to instructors using HCC Industries, Inc. (N9-189-096).

1990

Suggested Assignment Questions

1. Evaluate the decision to use "minimum performance standard"
    (MPS) targets instead of "stretch" targets.

2. Should HCC managers have expected that the MPS target-
    setting philosophy would be equally effective in all four
    operating divisions described?

3. What, if anything, could have been done to improve the
    implementation of the new philosophy?

Either of two articles can be assigned with the case as supple-
mentary reading. One describes conflicts among the multiple purposes for
which budgeting processes are used.[1] The other is more directive; it makes
the case that the choice of highly achievable budget targets, combined with
the proper selection of other management system elements, is optimal
(provides the best compromise) in most managerial situations.[2]

Question 1--MPS vs. Stretch Targets

HCC corporate managers' primary stated motivation for changing
their budgeting philosophy was their desire to improve the predictability
of corporate planning and financial reporting. They thought they could
improve corporate planning without compromising motivation. Motivation was
to be intact because the new system was designed to give division managers
a challenging target to shoot for, as well as an MPS, and no upside limits
on bonus potentials.

But if planning was the sole reason for change, corporate managers could have merely "factored down" the consolidation of the divisions'
plans. In other words, they could have taken a "negative reserve" to
protect against the consequences of some divisions not achieving their
plans.

Since the negative-reserve alternative is so obvious, there must
be something else going on. I think corporate managers had two other major
concerns. First, they were disturbed that some division managers were
adding overhead in periods when they are not achieving their targets and
when are earning bonuses for their performances. The division managers may not have treated the budget target as one that needed to be
achieved, and/or they may have been misled about the need for additional
resources by optimistic sales forecasts. Second, corporate managers did
not feel they had a good standard for evaluating whether their managers
were effective. They wanted a comparison with budget to signal when
control interventions were necessary (i.e., when a manager was not effective).

---

[1] M.E. Barrett and L.B. Fraser, "Conflicting Roles in Budgeting for
Operations," Harvard Business Review (November-December 1973).

[2] Merchant, K. A., "How Challenging Should Profit Budget Targets Be?"
Management Accounting (November 1990).

HCC's new budget/incentive system has some appealing features, but it seems to have failed in its early months for either of two related reasons. First, in an uncertain environment it is not possible to call any target 100% achievable, so the new system placed the division managers at risk of losing their jobs each year (at least in theory). They obviously were not comfortable with this risk.

The idea of less-than-100% achievability is illustrated in Figure TN-1. Expectations of actual performance are shown to be roughly symmetrical around a point B which can be labeled a "best guess." Budget targets can be set to provide a high probability that actual performance will be greater than the target, say point A. But even this low target does not provide a 100% likelihood that the target will be achieved.

The division managers' risk is heightened because the performance targets seem to be primarily top-down, even though they are derived from a negotiating process between the division managers and the COO. The COO seems not to have relented until he reached a number that he felt sure that an effective manager would be sure to achieve. But whose estimates are more realistic (see Exhibit 5)? A special note--the great disparity between the COO's and division manager's estimates in Sealtron stem from the fact that the COO did not feel the Sealtron manager (Lou Palamara) was effective, and he was setting him up to be replaced.

In class it can be noted that the "stretch" targets even in HCC's old system are far below point C on Figure TN-1, the 25-40% achievability level that some textbooks conclude provides the optimal motivation.[3] Mike Pelta in Hermetic Seal said he used to feel he had an 85-95% chance of achieving his targets (p. 8), but he also bragged that he had never missed a budget in his 33 years of being a manager. Carl Kalish in Glasseal felt the old probability was 90%. Thus even the old stretch targets were more highly achievable then best-guess targets. The question that can be raised in class is: Was/is motivation being compromised by these "excessively easy" targets?

The second cause of early failure of the new system seems to be that the operating managers' expected value of bonuses has declined sharply. Now they must exceed their MPS targets to earn bonuses, rather than merely exceed 60% of their stretch targets as before. But the division managers are not yet convinced that the MPS targets are that much easier to achieve than were the old stretch targets. For example, under each system, Kalish estimated his probability of achievement at 90%. So bonus expectations have been reduced, and the threat of the downside penalty of not achieving the targets has increased significantly.

Perhaps Al Berger (COO) knew that he would forgive the division managers if they failed to achieve their targets for reasons he felt were out of their control. If so, he failed to communicate this expectation throughout the HCC organization.

---

[3] For a review of this literature, see K. Merchant and J.-F. Manzoni, "The Achievability of Budget Targets in Profit Centers: A Field Study," The Accounting Review (July 1989), forthcoming.

It might be useful to put students in Al Berger's role to consid-
r how they would treat uncontrollable influences. Would they provide
orgiveness? (Doing so makes the corporation bear the risk; it makes the
udget somewhat 'flexible.') For example, try this scenario. If a major
overnment contract were canceled after a division's performance targets
ere set that adversely affected revenues (and profits) by, say, 20%:

1. Would they override the terms of the contract and provide
   some incentive compensation? If so, how much? (Estimate
   and forgive the full amount, or merely a token bonus?)

2. If uncontrollable influences caused a manager to miss many
   of the MPS, would they fire the manager? (This is an
   unlikely response.)

3. If forgiveness is to be given for events like this, how
   specific should the promises of forgiveness be before the
   measurement period begins? (Would such promises cause
   managers to appeal with a series of "excuses" at period-
   end?)

uestion 2--Any Differences Across Divisions?

While the divisions are in many ways quite similar, they have a
ew differences that perhaps should lead to special budgeting/evaluation/
eward differences.

a. Hermetic Seal is run by Mike Pelta. Mike is a powerful
   person in the corporation because he was a cofounder and is
   a major stockholder. Mike is also somewhat unique in that
   his philosophy toward budgeting seems to be to negotiate for
   a target he will be able to achieve. Can Al Berger, who is
   new in the company (hired in March 1987) negotiate as
   effectively with Mike Pelta as with the other division
   managers? (No.) Is replacing Pelta for not achieving MPS
   as significant a threat as it is for the other division
   managers? (No.)

b. Sealtron presents two unique considerations. First, the
   division missed its targets in 1987 and its personnel
   received no bonuses or salary increases. Lou Palamara
   (division manager) argues that this may cause employee
   retention problems. Should this type of employee retention
   issue have an effect on budgeting/evaluation/reward decisions? (Yes.)

   Second, corporate managers regard Lou Palamara as a poor
   manager. They feel that in 1987 Lou was inappropriately
   adding overhead (e.g., an industrial engineer and a production control manager) when his division was missing its
   budget targets. Lou is not convinced he was wrong. Cor-

porate managers want to signal to Lou that Sealtron financial performance is not satisfactory. If he fails to respond to that signal by not generating adequate results,
they want to set him up to be fired. Is that an appropriate
use of budget targets? (Yes.)

c. Hermetite is also unique in two ways. First, it is in a
turnaround situation, so planning uncertainty is high. As
Alan Wong (division manager) says in the case (p. 12),
nobody knows what to expect. How do you set budget targets
in such an environment?

Second, Alan Wong seems to be an inveterate optimist. (Alan
is not totally unique; I met and learned of other such
managers during my field interviews.) What causes some
managers to be optimistic? Personality? Situation? Is
Alan right when he says, 'If you don't set high standards,
you never achieve high performance (p. 11)?' (This is the
classic motivational argument.)

Question 3--Implementation

Several implementation problems have been discussed above.
Clearly division managers did not buy into the new system completely.

Other Questions that Might Be Raised in Class

1. Why do managers not play it straight in setting budget targets?

Most managers have multiple incentives to negotiate for an easy
target. They protect themselves against unforeseen contingencies, set
themselves up to earn bigger bonuses, and may free up resources that
they can use for discretionary purposes, thus increasing their autonomy.

Conversely, a few managers have incentives to negotiate for challenging targets. They may be signalling that they are aggressive and in
control and therefore should be trusted with additional resources (or
at least should keep their job for another year). Or they may be
honestly be asking to work toward a target that will provide them a
feeling of accomplishment.

2. A unique feature of HCC's new system is that corporate managers allow
the division managers to decide what their share of the division bonus
pool should be (p. 7). Is this a wise idea?

This feature was added to the contract because corporate managers felt
the various division managers contributed differently to the success
of their division. They did not want to dictate the reward proportions, so they let the division managers decide. They did discuss the
amount chosen with each manager and thought those discussions were
informative on both sides.

3. Why are bonus levels set where they are? Why 20-25% of base salary
    and not 10% or 100%?

    Bonus levels are set to provide a competitive total compensation
    package. They also reflect corporate philosophies about the level of
    risk managers should bear (and the rewards they should earn).

4. Why is there no upper cap on bonus possibilities?

    There is little good data on how many companies cap bonus potentials,
    but most seem to. (In my study of 12 firms,[4] nine firms used such
    caps.) Thus, HCC's practice seems unusual. The firms that use upper
    caps feel (1) the corporation should be protected against a windfall
    gain (a "bluebird") and against shortsighted behaviors by managers who
    want quick gains in the current period even at the risk of creating
    problems in future periods; (2) stability is more important than
    unsustainably high short-term growth and profitability; (3) division
    managers should not earn more than top management (vertical compensa-
    tion equity); and (4) compensation should be somewhat stable over
    time.

    HCC's deviation from normal practice stems directly from Andy
    Goldfarb's philosophy. He said, "I never cut off anybody's opportuni-
    ty. I've never understood that philosophy. The leverage for the
    company is so powerful."

5. Because of the significant penalties of not achieving the MPS targets,
    is there a danger that managers will attempt to carry profits across
    years?

    Some risk exists, obviously, but it is small because control is
    centralized. Division controllers report on a solid line basis to the
    corporate controller.

Subsequent Events

        Many significant events took place shortly after those described
in the case. First, Mike Pelta, the manager of Hermetic Seal was replaced
because he seemed incapable of delegating authority in order to develop his
management team. This lasted only a few months, as the division faltered
badly, and Mike was brought back in to fix the problems.

        Second, failures to meet the MPS targets caused both the chief
operating officer to be fired (in March 1988) and one division (Hermetite)
to be divested (in June 1988). About the Al Berger's (COO) firing, Andy
Goldfarb said: "He didn't live up to the terms of his contract. He signed
up and committed that these targets would be achieved. Those are the rules
we played by."

---

    [4] See K.A. Merchant, _Rewarding Results: Motivating Profit Center
Managers_ (Harvard Business School Press, 1989).

Third, Glasseal just failed to meet its MPS targets for FY 1988 because of major operating problems in its plating shop. But Carl Kalish was not replaced.

Fourth, Lou Palamara, the manager of Sealtron, had a heart attack and was removed from the day-to-day management of the business. During the year, this division had major problems meeting quality specifications on major government contracts, and Andy Goldfarb had to take over active management of the division to straighten out the problems.

Pedagogy

I suggest using an unstructured approach in teaching the case. Go right to the evaluation of the change. At some time it may be useful to clarify facts, such as about the key success factors, performance measures, and the budget negotiation process. And focus on the 'other questions' as they arise.

With about a half hour remaining, take an evaluative vote, and students will probably be split as to whether the problems were caused by the system design or its implementation. Then show the 15 minute videotape of Andy Goldfarb's comments. The videotape will undoubtedly provoke some additional discussion. It will also change some students opinions, and this change can be observed by asking for another evaluative vote.

Figure TN-1

Performance Expectations in an Uncertain Environment

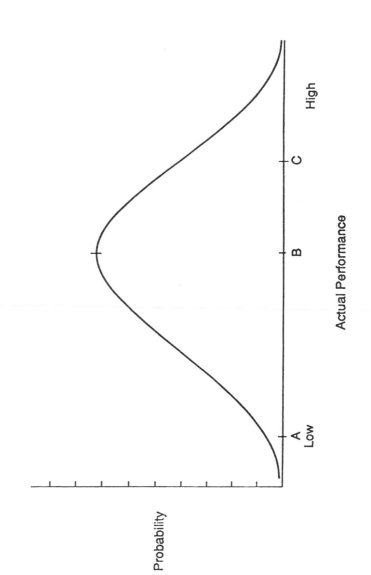

ES, INC.

Teaching Note

PURPOSE OF CASE

The ES, Inc. case raises the basic managerial issue as to what finan-cial measure(s) should be used for evaluating business unit plans and accomplishments. The case describes a company that is questionning the meaningfulness of the traditional accounting measures of performance (e.g., net income, return on investment). Company managers are in the early stages of considering whether or not a shareholder value model, which incorporates discounted cash flow principles, can be used to construct a better measure of performance. Thus, the case is useful for motivating a discussion of how to evaluate these two (and other) performance measures.

SUGGESTED ASSIGNMENT QUESTIONS

The following questions appear in the case (p. 9), and they been successful in guiding student preparation and class discussion:

1. Should ESI use "impact on shareholder value" as the primary financial criterion on which to evaluate:

    a. business unit plans,

    b. managerial accomplishments

2. If not, what criterion (or criteria) should be considered for each purpose? Should impact on shareholder value be considered at all?

3. If the impact on shareholder value criterion is used, how should the issues raised in the case be resolved?

THE EVALUATION OF PLANS QUESTION

Among MBA students, part (a) of question one, about how to evaluate business plans, should not be controversial. Most see "impact on share-holder value" as a useful criterion to use in evaluating business unit plans because the use of net present value models for evaluating capital expenditure proposals is fresh in their minds.

This teaching note was prepared by Assistant Professor Kenneth A. Merchant as an aid to instructors using the case ES, Inc. (9-183-061).

With executive students who have not studied finance recently, however, this issue can be very controversial, and considerable class time can be spent on discussing it. If this situation is likely, it may be necessary to discuss the case in two class periods, and either or both of the following articles can be assigned as background readings: Jack L. Treynor, "The Financial Objective in the Widely Held Corporation," Finan-cial Analysts Journal (March-April 1981), pp. 68-71; Alfred Rappaport, "Selecting Strategies that Create Shareholder Value," Harvard Business Review (May-June 1981), pp. 139-149. The Rappaport article is focused directly on the merits of using shareholder value models for strategic planning purposes.

THE MEASUREMENT OF PERFORMANCE QUESTION

While the planning issue is an important one which can be discussed at length, the case was actually written to raise the related performance measurement question: What should be used as the standard for judging managerial accomplishments? Two competing options are described in the case -- accounting and shareholder value measures of performance -- and the class discussion should revolve around the relative advantages and disadvantages of each.

If it is not clear from prior classes, I like to start the discussion by reminding students how important this measurement issue is. At managerial levels in most larger firms, "results-accountability" is the dominant form of control, as managers are generally allowing considerable autonomy but are held accountable for achieving certain results. Results accountability control requires: (1) defining the performance dimensions on which results are desired (e.g., profits, growth), (2) measuring performance on these dimensions, and (3) providing rewards (e.g., bonuses, promotions) to encourage the behaviors that will lead to the results desired.

The students' task is to compare the accounting and shareholder-value alternatives. It is possible to get right into the comparison, but I think it is useful to start by agreeing on a set of criteria to use for the comparison. When I first used this case, I started the class by having the students develop their own set of evaluation criteria, but that was a time-consuming process. Now I rely on a set of five criteria which are described in readings I have assigned previously: (1) congruence, (2) precision, (3) objectivity, (4) timeliness, and (5) understandibility. These criteria are discussed in detail in K. A. Merchant, "The Control Function of Management," Sloan Management Review (Summer 1982), pp. 43-55; and K. A. Merchant, Control in Business Organizations, Pitman, 1985. In this document, I will provide only a brief discussion of these criteria and an evaluation of the two ES, Inc. measurement alternatives, and two other alternatives--inflation accounting returns and operating cash flow--in terms of the criteria.

A. Congruence. It is congruence failures that have caused managers in ES, Inc. to consider adopting shareholder value measures of performance. Corporate staff personnel have observed that the company's returns to shareholders have not been closely associated with the company's performance as measured in accounting terms. They feel that measures derived from the shareholder value model (VALUmod) might provide better indicators of success, but they are still in the process of testing the model.

In theory, there is no question that shareholder value measures of performance are superior to accounting measures in terms of the congruence criterion.[1] If the primary financial goal of business firms is maximization of shareholder value, then measures of success should reflect changes in shareholder value. Any other measure is a surrogate, and there is considerable evidence that accounting measures of performance are very crude surrogates. Some of this evidence is anecdotal (e.g., Exhibits 5-8 of the ES case), but there have also been some large-scale empirical studies that have reached this conclusion.[2]

When the discussion about congruence comes up in the class, I help it along by providing a lecturette about why accounting measures of performance cannot be expected always to be highly correlated with changes in shareholder value changes. First, I put the general formula for calculating the value of an asset on the board:

$$V = \sum_{i} \frac{CF_1}{1+r} + \frac{CF_2}{(1+r)^2} + \ldots + \frac{CF_n}{(1+r)^n}$$

where   V = value
        CF = cash flow in period i;
        r = discount rate (includes real interest rate, allowance for
            inflation, and risk factor)

Since companies and divisions are assets from the point of view of the owners (shareholders), this is the formula for calculating the shareholder value of each of these entities.

With this formula in mind, it is easy to show why accounting measures of performance (AMP) and shareholder value changes should not be expected to be closely related:

-       AMP are primarily a summation of the effects of the transactions
        that took place during a given period. Most changes in value
        that do not result in a transaction are not recognized in income.

---

[1] To help ensure that students reach this conclusion, I assign the following one-page article: Alfred Rappaport, "New Measures of Executive Performance," Business Week (July 18, 1983), p. 15 (see Attachment 1).

[2] I discuss this point in detail and summarize this evidence in chapter 8 of my Control in Business Organizations monograph.

-   AMP are highly dependent on the choice of measurement method, and
    multiple measurement methods are often available to account for
    identical economic events (e.g., flowthrough vs. deferral of
    investment tax credits).

-   AMP are dependent on measurement rules that are sometimes heavily
    biased in favor of conservatism.

-   AMP ignore the economic worth of companies' intangible assets,
    such as research in progress, people, and the goodwill that has
    been built up.

-   AMP ignore the time value of money.

-   AMP ignore risk and changes in risk.

-   AMP focus on the past, and there is no guarantee that past
    performance is a reliable indicator of future performance.

Exhibit 5 and 6 of the case show specific examples of situations in
which AMP can be misleading, and it is important to make sure the students
understand how these situations can arise. Exhibit 5 shows an example of a
good investment that does not look good in accounting terms. Such a
situation occurs where an expenditure is expensed immediately or depreciat-
ed (amortized) more rapidly than the revenues generated from the expenditure or where the payoff (in accounting terms) toward the end of (or after)
the planning horizon. Exhibit 6 shows how a bad investment can look good
in accounting terms. This can occur where revenues appear early but
significant expenses are required after the end of the planning horizon.

The insight I want the students to reach is as follows. It is shareholder value that we want managers to increase. But when we observe that
managers have increased accounting income, we cannot be sure that they have
increased shareholder value. Thus, accounting measures of performance are
limited in their use as a measure of success or, in other words, the
"congruence" of accounting measures of performance is to be questioned.

B. Precision. Although shareholder value measures of performance are
superior in terms of congruence, this fact does not necessarily lead to the
conclusion that all firms should implement them because such measures do
not rate highly in terms of all the other criteria. Precision is one of
the criteria on which shareholder value measures rate poorly.

Precision refers to the accuracy with which a given quantity can be
measured. For precision to be high, the dispersion placed on a given
quantity by multiple, unbiased measurers would be small. If measures are
imprecise, neither managers nor subordinates will place much confidence in
them, and where imprecise measures are used for evaluation purposes,
managers run a high risk of misevaluating performance. The effect will
inevitably be negative reactions from those being evaluated as they will
see that, for example, equally good performance are rated differently.

The accounting measures of performance are clearly more precise than are the shareholder value measures. Accounting measures of performance focus primarily on transactions that have already taken place, and many measurement rules exist to limit the degree of discretion that can be applied to any economic event. Some imprecision is still present with accounting measures of performance as, for example, estimates must be made as to the collectability of receivables, but accounting precision is certainly high relative to that of shareholder value measures of performance. Forecasts of future cash flows and risk are subject to many different assumptions, such as to economic conditions, competitor actions, and the realizations of company successes, so the precision of shareholder value measures of performance is low.

C. Objectivity. Objectivity means freedom from personal bias. Here again, accounting measures of performance have an advantage. The accounting rules sharply limit the number of areas in which managers can impart biases to the numbers, which they tend to do usually in an optimistic direction. And where biases could exist, rigorous objectivity checks, done by experienced external and internal auditors limit the impact of the biases.

Shareholder value measures of performance are subject to considerable biases, as managers are likely to be very optimistic about future prospects, particularly if the amount of capital their entity is allocated or their compensation is affected by such optimism. To some extent upper management can provide a check on estimates of entity cash flow potentials, as they do now in evaluating expenditure proposals, but these checks are limited in effectiveness where lower-level managers have better information as to their own entities' prospects (as they should have in a decentralized organization).

D. Timeliness. Timeliness is not an issue in this comparison. Both measures are available on a timely basis.

E. Understandability. Understandability is a possible issue. Some students will argue that the shareholder value measures of performance are not easily understandable by line managers. If this is true, behavior will not be affected positively, and confusion and frustration will probably be inevitable.

Whether or not understandability is a problem depends on the managers, I think. Shareholder value measures are based on net present value principles, and well-trained, professional managers should already be familiar with them. The same is not true, of course, of less-highly-trained managers.

Summary. Attachments 1 and 2 to this note provide brief summaries of the evaluation of the measurement alternatives, first for evaluating top management and second for evaluating middle management. From this summary, it is clear that there is a dilemma. Congruence, which I feel is the single most important quality for a control system measure to have, is a potential problem with accounting measures of performance. Congruence is crucial because it is unproductive to define success in terms of a quantity

at is not meaningful, and in some situations, such as those shown in
hibits 5 and 6 of the case, accouting measures may even be counter-
oductive. I have labeled this problem of motivating people to produce a
antity which is not really what is wanted as "behavioral displacement";
is a direct effect of the lack of measurement congruence with true
ganizational goals.

Despite its definite advantages of the shareholder value measures in
erms of congruence, it is not clear that ES, Inc. should implement such
asures for control purposes, however. Such measures have precision and
jectivity problems that can be very serious, particularly if the measures
e used for allocating capital and compensation. Understandability could
so be a problem for some managers.

sues related to shareholder value measures

As discussed at the end of the case, the company has not fully devel-
ed its thinking about how the shareholder value measures might be imple-
ented. There are a number of unresolved issues, and it is useful to
scuss these in class.

One issue is whether the planning horizon should be extended. The
mpany's present practice is to assume that the operating cash flows in
e last year of the three year plan will remain constant in perpetuity.
is short horizon puts a lot of weight on the third year of the plan, but
his procedure may be adequate for some entities, such as those which
perate in relatively stable markets, which have many sales transactions in
given period, and which have relatively short product development cycles.
t a short horizon is not adequate for entities which are expecting
ignificant growth (cash flows are projected as flat after year 3), or
hose which will not derive the bulk of the incoming cash flows from their
urrent investments within the three year time period, perhaps because they
re investing in large amounts of fixed assets. In order to provide better
easures of the values and changes in values of these entities, it would
eem to be necessary that the company extend its planning horizon, perhaps
o five or seven years, or at least incorporate an assumption about a
rowth rate for projecting the cash flows out past the three-year horizon.

A second issue is whether plans should reflect a single point or some
orm of probability distribution. While the case can be made for consider-
ng probability distributions, it would probably be a very difficult idea
o implement because most managers are not experienced at estimating full
istributions. Thus it is probably best to leave this idea alone, at least
n the short term.

A third issue is how to include risk in the shareholder value model. This issue has been discussed extensively in the finance literature.[3] The options are as follows:

- Use the same discount rate for all entities.

- Estimate a risk factor based on the stock market betas of the closest competitors. This may be practicable if some pure-play competitors exist.

- Estimate a risk factor from some measures that are available, such as volatility in sales or earnings. This procedure is limited in that the historical ratios on which these indicators are based may not be valid in the future time periods being considered.

- Estimate future risk subjectively using all of the above indicators. The disadvantage of this procedure is that it would probably be very difficult to explain such estimates to the managers whose entities were being evaluated.

Option 2 is the theoretically correct choice, but the beta concept of risk may be difficult to explain to some managers, and pure-play competitors do not exist in many situations. The company is probably best advised to start with option 1, even though it is an inferior solution that will cause an overvaluation of risky entities and an undervaluation of less risky entities, and to experiment with the other options. Then they can experiment with options 2, 3 and 4 and decide over time if it is practical to try to make the model more accurate.

The fourth and fifth issues are how fast to involve managers in the process of developing and evaluating the shareholder value measures, and whether or not to link such measures to tangible organizational rewards. There is not enough information in the case to say much about these issues, but as they would involve quite a substantial change in the way managers think, it is likely that progress would have to be made relatively slowly.

OTHER MEASUREMENT ALTERNATIVES

As neither accounting nor shareholder value measures of performance satisfy all the measurement criteria, it is useful to get the class to think about what else might be done. I have listed the major alternatives

---

[3]See, for example, James C. Van Horne, "An Application of the Capital Asset Pricing Model to Divisional Required Returns," Financial Management (Spring 1980), pp. 14-19; Russell J. Fuller and Halbert S. Kerr, "Estimating the Divisional Cost of Capital: An Analysis of the Pure-Play Technique," The Journal of Finance (December 1981), pp. 997-1009; Benton E. Gup and Samuel W. Norwood III, "Divisional Cost of Capital: A Practical Approach," Financial Management (Spring 1982), pp. 20-24.

ere. A more detailed discussion of these options is included in chapter 8
f my control monograph.

1. Choose better accounting rules. There is no reason why the rules
   used for financial reporting have to be used for internal (control) purposes. Perhaps the company could improve congruence by
   capitalizing R&D, training, and advertising and sales promotion
   expenditures, or by implementing some form of inflation accounting.

2. Lengthen the measurement period. Accounting numbers are most
   limited in assessing performance in short periods of time.
   Annual and even biannual net income numbers may not be very
   meaningful; it depends on characteristics of the entity (e.g.,
   length of the production cycle, capital intensity). So perhaps
   rewards should be provided only for performance that is measured
   over a three year (or longer) period.

3. Use non-financial measures of performance. It may be possible to
   choose some non-financial indicators, such as market share,
   number of patents granted, or number of new customers, that
   provide better indications of success than do accounting numbers
   or shareholder value numbers.

ll of these options have some advantages and disadvantages. None would be
ated as excellent in terms of all of the evaluation criteria, as shown in
ttachments 1 and 2.

THE BOTTOM LINE

I have found that the discussion of this case varies significantly
epending on what has taken place in the preceding classes. When I used
his case directly after a series of cases which focused on accounting
easurement issues, the students were nearly unanimously against the
shareholder value concept. But when I used the case as a wrap-up case of a
section of the course on shareholder value measures of performance,[4] a
plurality of students thought ES, Inc. should go ahead with plans to expand
the use of the value model. This suggests to me that while the idea of
shareholder value measures of performance is seen as radical, continued
reflection about the issue leads some to conclude that its advantages
outweigh its disadvantages.

---

[4] I used Natomas North America (A)-(D) (9-184-031 through 034) and Acton
Life Insurance Company (9-109-042).

Attachment 1

EVALUATION OF FOUR MEASUREMENT ALTERNATIVES
FOR JUDGING TOP MANAGEMENT PERFORMANCE

Measurement Criterion	Measurement Alternative			
	Shareholder Returns	Accounting Returns	Infl.Acctg. Returns	Oper. Cash Flow
1. Congruence	excellent	qtrly-poor[4] annual-fair	?[4]	qtrly-poor[3] annual-fair (worse than acctg.)
2. Precision	excellent	good	fair	excellent
3. Objectivity	excellent	good	good	excellent
4. Timeliness	excellent	qtrly-good annual-fair	annual-fair	excellent
5. Understandability	good[1]	excellent	fair	excellent
6. Controllability[2]	fair	fair	fair	fair

1. May not understand how to influence.
2. If an important criterion, modify results measures: analysis of variance to separate out uncontrollable effects.
3. Easily manipulated.
4. Clearly better in some industries than others. Stable business with many transactions – good. Growing business with few transactions – poor.

Attachment 2

EVALUATION OF FIVE MEASUREMENT ALTERNATIVES
FOR JUDGING MIDDLE MANAGEMENT PERFORMANCE

	Measurement Alternative				
Measurement Criterion	Economic Return	Accounting Returns	Infl. Acctg. Returns	Oper. Cash Flow	KSF[1]
1. Congruence	excellent	qtrly-poor annual-fair	?	qtrly-poor annual-fair (worse than acctg.)	excellent
2. Precision	poor	good	fair	excellent	varies[2]
3. Objectivity	fair	good	good	excellent	
4. Timeliness	excellent	qtrly-good	annual-fair	excellent	
5. Understandability	excellent	fair	fair	fair	excellent

1. Key success factors (p.89 Anthony and Dearden).
   Important in explaining success or failure of an organization.

2. (e.g. market share data may not be available).
   Customer satisfaction difficult to measure, quality, backlog, and
   production yield good.